THE SHEFFIELD COOKBOOK
BACK FOR THIRDS

All Vegan
Shelf (VG)
Pick & Mix
£4.50
(Gelatine Free)
HOT CHOCOLATE STIRRERS - £3.50
CHOCOLATE DROPS - £3.50
CHOCOLATE LOLLIES - £3.50
DARK ORANGE SHARDS
Limited Edition SHARDS
Rocky Road
Cookies & Cream
Chocolate Shards

THE SHEFFIELD COOK BOOK - BACK FOR THIRDS

First edition printed in 2022 in the UK

ISBN: 978-1-915538-02-4

Written by: Ash Birch, Katie Fisher, Joe Food & Lizzie Morton

Photography by: Timm Cleasby & Ellie Grace

Designed by: Phil Turner & Paul Cocker

Sales & PR: Emma Toogood & Lizzy Capps

Contributors: Lis Ellis, Nick Hallam, Tim Green

me:ze PUBLISHING

Published by Meze Publishing Limited
Unit 1b, 2 Kelham Square
Kelham Riverside
Sheffield S3 8SD
Web: www.mezepublishing.co.uk
Telephone: 0114 275 7709
Email: info@mezepublishing.co.uk

Printed in Great Britain by Bell & Bain Ltd, Glasgow

WELCOME BACK FOR THIRDS

In 2014, we began a series of regional cookbooks with a celebration of Sheffield's amazing independent food and drink scene. Since then, things have developed so much that we've put together not one but two more editions to showcase more of the brilliant cafes, restaurants, producers, pubs, coffee shops, bars and bakeries that grace our city.

With more than 50 recipes to try at home, plus wine and beer pairings recommended by Sheffield's own Tenaya Wines and Industry Tap, this book is just as packed with culinary goodness as the first two. We think that food and drink tastes better when you know how much love and dedication goes into it, so we've caught up with all the lovely people who generously shared their signature dishes, desserts and cocktails to tell their stories too.

For those in the know, it's hard to beat Sheffield's incredible array of small businesses, whether you're after a pie and a pint or a fine dining experience. Many are run by families and artisans who are not just about turning a profit but creating the best food and drink they possibly can. Often they'll use ingredients grown, reared, distilled and produced within the city or its surrounding countryside, creating a network of supportive independents who collaborate and innovate.

One thing we all have in common is the pride in what Sheffield is, has been, and can become. And what better way to be part of that exciting future than indulging in everything the Steel City has to offer? If you are new to these parts and can only associate us with football or The Full Monty, it's time to get stuck in. For locals, here's a reminder of all the top scran on our doorstep.

We invite you to cook from this book but also to get out there and support the businesses that made it possible: eat, drink and enjoy our wonderful hometown.

TEAM MEZE X

CONTENTS

A FAMILY BUSINESS

Born from the life experiences and shared culinary passions of mother and daughter duo Jane and Alexa, Aesthete offers the people of Sheffield a taste of culinary delights from around the world.

Jane and Alexa opened Aesthete in 2015, bringing with them the cuisine and cultural influences of Greece after living there for 20 years. Alexa had experience as a barista and a baker, and Jane as a chef, so they combined their skills as mother and daughter to open a family-run café and bistro. By 2022, they had expanded to three different locations in Sheffield: Crookesmoor, Walkley and Crosspool.

Aesthete is unique in the way it fuses some of the best cuisines around the world, with a focus on Mediterranean cuisine. At the same time, their cakes and desserts can range from a Greek galaktoboureko (custard pie) and Victoria sponge, to a vegan Nutella Gateau (recipe included in this chapter) and a berry streusel cheesecake. Each venue has its own menu and offers different dishes, making each location a unique experience. The venues update their menus every year, as well as offering a variety of seasonal specials, such as hearty Greek stews in the winter and refreshing Italian avocado bruschetta in the summertime.

Alexa and Jane highly value a homely atmosphere and an uplifting, welcoming decor, and they carefully manage and design the space of their shops themselves. An Aesthete (pronounced es-theet) is one who has an unusually high sensitivity to beauty in art and nature. Jane and Alexa made sure to incorporate this when it came to designing the restaurant, so the interior promotes natural sunlight with large windows, an open space and a relaxing ambience. Aesthete is intended to accommodate anything from a catch-up brunch to private events, as well as offering bespoke cakes for all occasions.

Aesthete would not be as successful without their hardworking and dedicated staff, who put as much effort and passion into the business as Alexa and Jane do. Catering for such worldly tastes means that Aesthete has unique demands of those they employ because the food and service provided isn't typically part of their past experiences. Everyone on the team rises to the occasion though, and both Jane and Alexa are incredibly proud that they have adapted and overcome. The team truly represent Aesthete at its best, building relationships with customers who soon become regulars. It's also thanks to the support of Sheffield's community which has allowed Aesthete to become a huge success.

Aesthete
OPEN

NUTELLA GATEAU

Preparation time: 30 minutes, plus 1 hour chilling | Cooking time: 35-40 minutes | Serves 12-16

As an immense lover of chocolate, Alexa spent years researching the perfect chocolate cake recipe, aiming for the perfect balance of sweetness, moisture and chocolatiness. Aesthete's signature "Nutella" Gateau ticks all these boxes, on top of being dairy-free and vegan!

For the sponge

600ml soy milk
175ml sunflower oil
4 tbsp white wine vinegar
625g caster sugar
410g plain flour
85g cocoa powder
1½ tsp baking powder
1½ tsp bicarbonate of soda

For the buttercream

250g Stork (or any type of margarine), at room temperature
430g icing sugar
70g cocoa powder
2 tbsp hazelnut praline
Soy milk, optional

To decorate

Chopped hazelnuts
Dried flower petals

For the sponges

Preheat the oven to 170°c and line or grease two 22cm cake tins.

In a bowl, add all the wet ingredients and whisk together until the mixture becomes thick and curdly – this is what you want it to look like – it may not look very appealing at this stage, but it will come together at the end! Set the bowl aside.

In another bowl, add all the dry ingredients, and mix. Add the wet mixture to the dry ingredients and whisk well together to ensure it is all combined and that there are no lumps. Divide and pour the batter in the two cake tins. Place in a preheated oven and bake for 35-40 minutes.

For the buttercream

Beat the Stork, cocoa powder, and icing sugar for a couple of minutes, then add the hazelnut praline. If the buttercream is a bit stiff and doesn't have a spreadable consistency, add a splash of soy milk to soften it up.

To assemble and decorate

Once the sponges have cooled down, using a palette knife, spread a third of the buttercream on the first layer of cake, place the second layer of cake on top and spread another third of the buttercream over the top and sides too, making sure it is all covered. For a smooth buttercream finish, we always crumb-coat our cakes and place them in the fridge for an hour, or until set, and then we repeat the process with the remaining buttercream.

Don't forget to save some of the buttercream to decorate the cake with; you can use any nozzle you have, so get creative! Finish by sprinkling the chopped hazelnuts and dried flower petals on top.

A SEAT AT THE TABLE

In 2016, husband and wife Mario Masia and Giovanna Casiddu opened Akentannos – Sheffield's first restaurant specialising in Sardinian cuisine on the vibrant Sharrow Vale Road.

Sardinia is the first ever declared Blue Zone, where a larger part of the population (compared to other countries) lives up to 100 years old! The term Akentannos (a-chent'-annos), is a traditional Sardinian greeting that means 'may you live to be 100', so that could not be more appropriate.

The strength of Mario and Giovanna's restaurant comes from the quality of their raw ingredients that revive the flavours of the Sardinian tradition in today's products. It's also in their preservation and love for good food and respecting cooking times, all in order to enhance the aromas and true taste of Sardinia. The pair pride themselves on using the finest and freshest ingredients. To keep the tastes as true to the Sardinian influence as possible, the majority of said ingredients are imported from Sardinia directly, but then for the remainder they'll source locally wherever possible.

There's an expression in 'Sardo' – "sa cughina minore no timede su fuste" which translates to "simple cuisine makes the home great." This is the philosophy Akentannos live by and is a perfect ethos for those who love the land of sun and blue sea, full of natural fragrances and intense flavours. The team are forever striving to cook authentic and innovative Sardinian food which, in their view, is the best of the old and the new, all served to you in their friendly atmosphere. At Akentannos, they offer a wide choice of unique culinary products, capable of satisfying even the most demanding palates. Mario, also the head chef, conjures up a wide variety of unique culinary delights on the daily. Being celiac himself, he takes great care to provide plenty of gluten-free options for customers to enjoy. With each dish prepared on the spot, you can be guaranteed everything is served fresh.

Recently, the restaurant was rewarded for its exceptionally high standards by being recognised in the UK Enterprise Awards. They were also bestowed the title of Best Italian Restaurant 2022 – South Yorkshire!

From Mario and Giovanna themselves, "we hope to take you away from today's hectic lifestyle and offer you a table in Sardinia."

SOPRASOLE
PALA

FREGOLA AI FRUTTI DI MARE

Preparation time: 20 minutes, plus 2 hours draining | Cooking time: 25 minutes | Serves 4

This typical Sardinian pasta owes its name to the Latin term "ferculum", which means "crumb". The fregola is in fact obtained by mixing the semolina flour with warm water and salt with quick gestures. This way small crumbs are obtained which are then toasted in the oven.

250g clams
250g mussels
2 squid
250g red shrimp
1 medium onion
4 tbsp extra virgin olive oil
300g fregola sarda
320g salmon
4 king prawns
1 glass of white wine
2 tbsp organic lemon zest
200g tomato sauce
1litre vegetable broth
20g bottarga

Put the clams in cold water for at least 2 hours to let them drain, and then rinse well. Next, clean the mussels and rinse well, and then for the squid, remove the skin and entrails, then rinse well and cut into rings. With the red shrimp, clean them from the head to the carapace and remove the vein – the black line running down the shrimp's back.

Cut the onion into chunks and brown it in a large pan with a drizzle of oil, then add the fregola sarda. Toast the pasta for a few minutes then add the squid, mussels and clams, salmon, red shrimps, and the whole king prawns. Leave everything to flavour and then add in the white wine and lemon zest. Finally, add the tomato sauce and proceed to cook over a low heat as if it were a risotto for about 20 minutes. Add the vegetable broth whenever the fregola requires it.

Complete with grated bottarga and lemon zest and serve.

CERVO ALLE ERBE AROMATICHE

Preparation time: 5 minutes | Cooking time: 5 minutes | Serves 2

Venison has a typically wild and decisive flavour; it is usually characterised by a pleasant sweetish aftertaste. Here, we've made the decision to use aromatic herbs and pecorino cream to best enhance its taste and make it appreciable even to those who are tasting it for the first time.

3 rosemary sprigs
3 sage sprigs
3 thyme sprigs
Extra virgin olive oil
2 venison fillets

Put the herb sprigs in a pan with a little oil and heat for about a minute. Add the venison fillets and cook them until they're rare.
Serve with a cream of Cacio e Pepe Sardinian pecorino cheese. Enjoy!

BREWING UP THE NEXT BIG THING

Endlessly customisable and always bang on trend, the bubble tea at ALS Gongcha is taking Sheffield by storm!

ALS Gongcha serves authentic Taiwanese bubble tea from a stylish café in central Sheffield and a street food stall in Cutlery Works. The franchise originated in Taiwan, and Kelvin Quick, who is also the owner of Sheffield's Szechuan restaurant China Red, runs the Sheffield branch of ALS Gongcha. He is passionate about bringing the latest bubble tea trends from East to West and always on the lookout for popular products and new ideas to embrace.

The name refers to the Taiwanese origins of the tea leaves, with ALS being short for Alishan where they are grown, and gongcha meaning 'emperor's tea' to reflect the finest quality of the produce. Most bubble tea starts with these tea leaves being brewed in hot water, then this base is customised to make a hot or cold drink with the sweetness level and milk of your choice. ALS Gongcha offers a huge range of options for creating your perfect drink, alongside the standard menu to help those who are new to the bubble tea phenomenon!

The tea itself ranges from black and green to matcha and oolong, with plant-based and dairy milks available to suit most dietary requirements. Bubble tea comes with tapioca balls – the soft and squishy 'bubbles' that give the drink its name – but these can be left out according to personal preference. Kelvin has found that people are generally happy to try the more adventurous options, so much so that the top seller is currently a sweetened milky tea with a lightly cheese-flavoured cream on top. This is one of the newest imports from China, where bubble tea is a huge hit, and demonstrates that it can include almost any flavourings, from red beans to crème brulée.

The cafe offers takeout teas as well as plenty of space to sit in, with a relaxing atmosphere and floral feature wall that's proved very popular with Instagrammers! Kelvin aims to continue expanding the venture and is soon branching out into desserts alongside the bubble tea, including freshly made waffles and sweet treats sourced from the Yorkshire-based producer Just Desserts. Situated next to the Hallam University area of the city on Eyre Street, ALS Gongcha is a great spot for students as well as anyone wanting to try the next big thing in bubble tea!

ALS
GONGCHA
阿里山贡茶

ALS GONGCHA ALS GONGCHA
阿里山贡茶
ALS GONGCHA 贡

Classic Milk Tea Series
Als Latte Series
Fruit Tea Series
Smoothie Series
Japanese Matcha Series

NO
SMOKING & VAPING
Chupa Chups
ALS GONGCHA
FOOD ALLERGIES

ALSGONGCHA
红茶
绿茶
阿里山乌龙茶
四季春
奶茶
GONGCHA Als GONGCHA

ALS
GONGCHA
阿里山贡茶

ALSGONGCHA

PANDA FRUIT TEA

Preparation time: 10 minutes | Serves 1

Refresh your summer with this Taiwanese iced drink based on green tea and sweetened with honey. Quick and easy to make, it's a great alternative to the typical British or American iced tea.

1 tbsp tapioca pearls
1 tbsp kanten jelly
2 slices of lime
450ml green tea
60ml passionfruit concentrate
20ml longan honey
Ice

You will need a cocktail shaker, measuring jug and large serving glass for this recipe.
Put the tapioca pearls, kanten jelly and lime slices into the glass.
Pour the green tea into the shaker, then add the passionfruit concentrate, honey and some ice.
Shake the mixture until cold, then pour into the glass and serve.

ALSGONGCHA

INSPIRED BY INDIA, MADE IN SHEFFIELD

As one of the oldest Indian restaurants in the city, Ashoka is known across Sheffield for its 'reyt good curreh' and unfailingly warm welcome.

Ashoka was established on Ecclesall Road in 1967 by Kamal Ahmed, a young Bengali who had no industry experience except waiting tables – he used to order tea at The Savoy to watch and learn the art of service – but was able to introduce the real flavours of Indian cooking to the neighbourhood long before multiculturalism entered the mainstream. Kamal went on to produce chilled ready meals in a Parkway factory which were sold to the likes of Harrods and Waitrose in the 80s, as well as opening two other restaurants in Sheffield and Dore. Over the years he trained both front and back of house staff, many of whom went on to own their own restaurants in Sheffield and beyond.

Since Kamal's retirement in 2004, the business has been in the hands of Rahul Amin, who has continued to focus on always getting the basics right: a delicious plate of food, served by friendly people in a comfortable environment. In addition to good hospitality, Ashoka has always had a flair for standing out in the crowd. From handwritten calligraphy on the menus and Sheffield-made silver cutlery in the early days, to the unique Taxi Driver curry created by the restaurant, they know how to do things a little differently.

In 2020, Ashoka underwent a refurbishment inspired by the cafes of Mumbai and now features a monochrome tiled floor, tiffin boxes and wooden tables. These classic touches make it feel homely, yet unlike most other curry houses, and the menu reflects this too. Karai, kashmiri and biryani jostle for diners' attention alongside lamb chops, chicken tikka and butter naans from the traditional charcoal tandoor. Their drinks list, menu and service style is distinct to them, although it has inspired many other restaurants in the city over the years, and Ashoka remains a unique place thanks to its heritage in Sheffield.

Ashoka has been featured on The Times' list of best curry houses in Britain and named in the Good Food Guide, but the biggest testament to its enduring success are the customers. Rahul and the team are grateful for each and every diner, from those who were there on opening day to first time visitors. Consistency is key for any successful restaurant, with a touch of innovation, and that's why the past 55 years have been amazing for Ashoka. Their experiences have made the staff, food and the restaurant better with each passing day. Let's look forward to many more years of delicious food and drink which is inspired by India and made in Sheffield.

JIVAN SANJIVANI
CHHATRISHA & CO.
Parle-G
VinayaK
ROSE DHOOP STICKS
LAXMI DHOOP

Diet
PARATHA

REYT GOOD CURREH
WWW.ASHOKA1967.COM

WHITE WINES
BEERS

ASHOKA
INSPIRED BY INDIA ◆ MADE IN SHEFFIELD
REYT GOOD CURREH

EASY RESTAURANT STYLE MALAI CHICKEN TIKKA

Preparation time: 10 minutes, plus 24 hours marinating | Cooking time: 15 minutes | Serves 4

This slightly different chicken tikka is deliciously moreish. We tried to keep the ingredients simple to encourage people to make and enjoy it! The Mr Naga Pickle isn't essential but once you've tasted it, we think it'll be a pantry staple.

For the spiced mango salad

2 mangoes (firm and tart)
1 sweet red pepper, ½ red onion
2 hot small green chillies
Handful of cherry tomatoes
¼ cucumber, 1 bullet chilli
10 fresh mint leaves
¼ bunch of coriander
1 tsp olive oil,½ lime

For the green chutney

1 bunch of coriander
2.5cm fresh ginger, 2 cloves of garlic
2 small green chillies
2 tsp lemon juice, 1 tsp caster sugar
¾ tsp ground cumin
½ tsp salt, or to taste

For the malai chicken tikka

4 chicken breasts, diced
2 tbsp each grated mature cheddar cheese and natural yoghurt
1 tbsp each single cream and fresh ginger paste
1 tsp each plain flour and Mr Naga Chilli Pickle
4 green bird's eye chillies
2 cloves of garlic
1 tsp cracked black pepper, ¼ tsp salt

For the spiced mango salad

First, prepare all the ingredients. Deskin and dice the mango, deseed and dice the red pepper, dice the red onion, finely slice the fresh green chilli and quarter the cherry tomatoes. Dice and deseed the cucumber, squeezing lightly to remove excess water content. Finely dice the bullet chilli, leaving the seeds in or taking them out to suit your preferred heat level. Combine all the ingredients in a bowl with a pinch of ground cumin and salt. Mix well and then squeeze in the lime juice to finish.

For the green chutney

Grind all the ingredients together with a pestle and mortar or in a food processor until well blended. This chutney can be made ahead and frozen in small portions.

For the malai chicken tikka

Combine all the ingredients in a bowl so the chicken pieces are completely coated, then cover and place in the fridge. For best results, marinate the chicken for 24 hours.

To cook the chicken, preheat the oven to 180°c fan and line a baking tray with foil. Place the marinated chicken tikka pieces on the tray, spaced apart, and cook for 10 minutes.

Turn the chicken pieces over, brush on any remaining marinade, then cook for another 5 minutes. Remove from the oven and leave to rest for 5 minutes.

This next step is optional but delicious; put the cooked chicken in a bowl, add a tablespoon of melted butter and toss until coated.

Serve the chicken tikka with your spiced mango salad and green chutney.

WINES
4.95 (175ml) / 16.50
5.50 (175ml) / 17.95 (Bottle)
04. VIOGNIER, LE
(175ml) / 17.95 (Bottle)
27.95 (Bottle)
59.95 (Bottle)
11. PROSECCO - MINI BOTTLE (APPROX 2 FLUTES) North Italy 8.00 (200ml) (Bottle)
SAN PELLEGRINO SPARKLING 3.50
ACQUA PANNA STILL 3.50
4.8% Bold classic IPA
SAN MIGUEL 0.0%
Alcohol free lager beer
FRUIT JUICES
Pineapple / Apple /
COKE / DIET COKE
Please note that a service charge is not included in your final bill. All gratuities are split between the team who served you today.

BEHIND THE DOOR

With French-Polynesian influences, and a beautiful décor of flowers, huts, and of course bamboo, Sheffield's first Tiki bar opened its doors in 2014.

Owner David Pickard wanted to open somewhere that would pay homage to and truly appreciate the flavours and delights the Tiki term inspires, so he created Bamboo Door. The decoration is inspired by his travels to Caribbean islands, where he has tried to bring something from each trip to add unique design ideas that are not normally seen in bars. It's the perfect locale for a midweek date, whilst also being a lively party venue at the weekends, with DJs and blow torches making it the place to be to blow off steam. Everybody on the team plays an important part in ensuring the customers' experiences are unforgettable. They'll go out of their way to make every request thrown at them, no matter how wild it sounds – if they've got the ingredients, they'll make it. Sometimes those weird concoctions turn out to be unexpected winners too! For those new to the cocktail scene, the staff are more than happy to recommend something they think will be a hit, based on your preferences.

As well as customer satisfaction, sustainability is another top priority for the team at Bamboo Door. Understanding the importance of doing their bit for the planet, they've ensured their practices are as environmentally friendly as possible. This includes sourcing their spirits from a local supplier – Avant Garde – and minimising their food waste through dehydrating their own fruit. They've also found innovative ways to reduce their plastic usage, like replacing their plastic stirrers with real shells that can be taken home or be washed and reused. The plastic straws from their Hibiscuous Girl have also been replaced with banana leaves and edible flowers, which not only keeps the theme, but also adds a pretty quality to the drink!

Bamboo's core menu changes every couple of years, with fruity drinks that pack a punch being guaranteed. Regularly taking the top spot among visitors, Mangoes in a Bar is definitely a firm favourite. Turtle Killer Qu'est-ce C'est – a punny play on the song title Psycho Killer – and Hibiscuous Girl are both popular with the staff too. Fresh specials menus and regular brand events happening throughout the year ensure that customers are kept on their toes for what will come next.

With discounts for fellow hospitality workers already in place, Bamboo are hoping to implement a new scheme by the end of September, whereby on Friday nights, that same discount will be extended to anyone that works in Sheffield. Coined Pau Hana, which roughly translates to "going for a drink after work", this will be Bamboo's way of showing their appreciation for the local worker, so make sure to head on down!

ALOHA
Bamboo Door
TIKI COCKTAIL BAR

WHAT A LOVELY PEAR

Preparation time: 10 minutes | Serves 1

Lovely Pear was created to use fresh ingredients and interesting tropical flavours using the lychee. The pear purée was used as it is less artificially sweet and the texture creates a nice mouthfeel to the drink. The use of pear was also our take on dessert/pastry inspired beverages. The What A Lovely Pear was a Bamboo Door drink from back in 2017 and has only recently been retired from the core menu.

25ml vodka
25ml lychee liqueur
20ml lemon juice
20ml pear purée (blend a tin of pear halves with the syrup they are preserved in)
20ml passionfruit syrup
80ml lychee juice

Shake well and strain over cubed ice with a slice of lemon to garnish. If you used a fresh lemon for the juice you can just take a slice from there – we're all about limiting our waste over here!
Optional - add a crushed cap for a touch of Tiki style.

FRESH TO DEATH

Preparation time: 5 minutes | Serves 1

Fresh to Death is a punny twist from the song So Fresh, So Clean by Outkast, and was created to offer the classic piña colada vibe without the heaviness of all the cream. You don't often see piña colada style flavour profiles with a vodka base which we thought was a good entry point for people who enjoy that coconut and pineapple flavour combo but maybe aren't into their rum yet.

50ml pineapple vodka
20ml lime juice
20ml coconut purée (Coco Re'al or Coco Lopez works best)
80ml pineapple juice

Shake well and strain over cubed ice with a slice of pineapple to garnish.
Optional – add a crushed cap for a touch of Tiki style.

COMMUNAL DRINKING AND DINING

Based in Nether Edge, Bench has been through quite a journey to become established in Sheffield's dining scene thanks to the dedication and innovation of its owners.

Bench started life as a side project for owners Jack and Ronnie back in 2018, alongside their day jobs at Public, where they were part of the team that won Observer Food Monthly's best place to drink in the UK 2018. They hosted three sold out pop-ups in some of their favourite independent businesses around Sheffield with nights in diverse settings from flower shops to design studios. The focus of these evenings was communal drinking and dining, with the food centred around open fire cooking, and the drinks closing the divide between bar and kitchen, always sharing and pairing ingredients.

After their huge success as a pop-up, it was the right time to find a more permanent place to call home and their bistro, bar and wine shop 'Bench' opened in October 2020 in the Nether Edge neighbourhood. The name is quite literal, referring to the bench in the centre of the dining area which creates a relaxed atmosphere in the friendly venue. The regularly changing seasonal small plate menu focuses on British produce and cooking over open fire, with natural wines and cocktails to accompany your meal.

The pork collar steak dish in particular has become a staple. "We are big fans of this cut of meat, because you get different textures throughout with lovely fat content," explains Jack. "It's an underrated cut which we feel doesn't get the praise it deserves." The pork collar steak is paired with Bench's own version of XO sauce (usually a spicy seafood sauce from Asia) which uses charcuterie offcuts. Bench sources all its cured meats from Curing Rebels, a small artisan producer based in Brighton who champion British produce and all things cured and smoked.

Following the initial launch in October 2020, Bench was forced to close due to Covid restrictions just two weeks after opening. However, Jack and Ronnie promptly turned their hand to takeaways by launching Feathers Fried Chicken which saw them through the difficult months. They also founded a natural wine subscription service which is still a thriving business in its own right. Since re-opening in the April 2021, the team have gone on to win Exposed Magazine's Best New Restaurant award and are proud to be serving up their neighbourhood vibes and delicious seasonal food to Sheffield.

OPEN

GRILLED PORK COLLAR STEAK WITH REBEL XO

Preparation time: 30 minutes | Cooking time: 30 minutes, including resting | Serves 2

We are big fans of pork collar steak, because you get different textures throughout with lovely fat content. It's an underrated cut which we feel doesn't get the praise it deserves. For the XO sauce, you can substitute the charcuterie offcuts for any minced meat or charcuterie.

For the pork

60g salt
40g sugar
1litre water
2 x 150g pork collar steaks

For the Rebel XO

175ml vegetable oil
1 shallot, minced
15g Korean red pepper flakes
15g garlic, thinly sliced
15g ginger, thinly sliced
2 star anise
1 piece of cassia bark
150g Curing Rebel's charcuterie offcuts, minced
30ml light soy sauce
30g shallot, sliced and fried until golden brown
30g garlic, sliced and fried until golden brown

For the sauce

100ml good quality chicken stock
50g Rebel XO (see above)
30g cold butter
10ml sherry vinegar
5g flat leaf parsley, finely sliced

For the pork

Dissolve the salt and sugar in the water, then add whatever aromats you like, have lying about, or go well with pork, such as hard herbs like sage or rosemary and whole spices like star anise or fennel seeds. Place the pork snugly in a container and pour over the brine. Any brine that's left over can be kept and used again. Leave for 2-3 hours depending on the thickness of the steak.

Once the pork is brined, remove and pat dry. Grill on a barbecue until just pink in the middle. Alternatively, you can use a standard grill or cook the pork in a pan with lots of foaming butter, garlic and herbs. Make sure you rest the meat for a good amount of time, then slice it ready for eating.

For the Rebel XO

Heat two thirds of the oil in a saucepan, then add the minced shallot and cook out. Add the chilli flakes and cook for 1 minute, then stir in the garlic, ginger, star anise and cassia bark. Turn the heat up high, stirring continually, and add the charcuterie offcuts. Cook everything together for 2-3 minutes until nicely coloured.

Add the remaining oil and turn the heat down, then leave the mixture to cook out for 30 minutes. Remove the pan from the heat and cool. Once cooled, remove the whole spices and stir in the soy sauce, fried shallots and fried garlic. Pulse with a stick blender until you have a thick ragu-like texture.

For the sauce

Bring the chicken sauce to a gentle simmer, then stir in the Rebel XO. Add the cold butter and keep stirring until the sauce is glossy and a good consistency. Finish with the sherry vinegar and parsley, then taste to check whether it needs any more seasoning.

Pour the sauce over and around the pork steak. Serve with steamed or grilled green veg.

GOING FOR GOLD

Bullion are Yorkshire's first 'bean-to-bar' artisan chocolate maker, running a factory space in Neepsend and an all-day café/bar at Cutlery Works food hall.

A self-professed foodie from a young age, Max Scotford first started making chocolate as a hobby while at university, using a small spice grinder to experiment with different cacao origins and flavour notes. As this interest deepened, Max began to see a gap in the market for a Sheffield-based craft chocolate company, one which would import cocoa beans from all over the world and make their bars truly from scratch.

Bullion launched in 2016, beginning its journey from a small 200 sq ft workshop in Neepsend. It was then a case of building up the brand, perfecting the core range, making contacts, encouraging local places to stock their products, and, perhaps most importantly, helping to spread the word of bean-to-bar chocolate across the UK. They quickly exceeded expectations: Bullion won a Silver Prize in the Academy Chocolate Awards and added the likes of Harvey Nichols and John Lewis to a growing client list.

In 2018, the company joined Cutlery Works, the largest food hall in the north of England, a move which provided a larger production space as well as the opportunity to branch out into baked goods, hot drinks and cocktails. The company's stock as a Sheffield brand grew significantly, and as a result they focused on expanding their product range via collabs with other local makers: coffee liqueur with Locksley Distilling, chocolate stouts with several local breweries and their hugely popular scented candles made from cocoa husk by Yorkshire Candle Co.

While a national lockdown was challenging, it also saw considerable online growth for Bullion - so much so, in fact, that they were able to open a bigger factory space in Neepsend, repurposing the Cutlery Works production unit into a cosy café-cum-cocktail-bar. Keen to share their passion for craft chocolate with customers, they regularly host public tours, events and tasting experiences across both venues.

The ultimate dream is to one day unite factory and café/bar into a flagship site offering the ultimate Bullion experience, but until then the focus remains on staying true to their early ethos: using natural ingredients to create award-winning, ethically sourced chocolate, resulting in a pure bar of something truly worth treasuring.

BULLION
CRAFT CHOCOLATE
COFFEE
ESPRESSO 2.6
LONG BLACK 3
FILTER 3
FLAT WHITE 3.2
CAPPUCCINO 3.2
LATTE 3.2
syrup +.5
alternative milk +.5
HOT CHOCOLATE
HALLMARK 3.7
Our take on the classic using our house dark or milk chocolate
MOCHA 4.5
Caravan coffee meets Bullion chocolate
SIGNATURE 4.5
Select one of our award-winning bars from the counter and we'll do the rest!
TEA
YORKSHIRE 2.6
BAKED GOODS
SEE COUNTER
Proudly serving
CARAVAN
COFFEE ROASTERS
Our Cow Molly
Daily Blend

BULLION
SMALL BATCH
Dark
MADAGASCAR
Milk
CHOCOLATE
44% ECUADOR
SANTO DOMINGO
NET WT

BULLION
2016
CHOCOLATE
MAKERS

BULLION BROWNIE

Preparation time: 40-45 minutes | Cooking time: 30-35 minutes | Makes 12-15

Who doesn't love a gooey chocolate brownie with a perfectly crisp crust? The rich flavour of top quality dark chocolate makes these a real treat for any occasion.

220g unsalted butter, plus a touch more for greasing
340g dark chocolate (70% cocoa), coarsely chopped
370g sugar
4 large eggs
1 1/2 tsp pure vanilla extract
185g plain flour
1/4 tsp sea salt

Preheat the oven to 180°c. Butter a 23 by 33cm (or similar) baking tray, then line with greaseproof paper.

In a medium pan, add enough water to reach a few centimetres up the sides. Set a medium bowl on top, making sure that the bottom of the bowl does not touch the water. Bring the water to a boil. Add the butter and 140g of the chocolate to the pot. Heat while stirring and scraping down the sides frequently until completely melted. Remove the bowl and set aside to cool slightly for around 10 minutes.

Whisk the sugar into the cooled chocolate mixture.. Add the eggs and vanilla, then whisk until the mix starts to pull away from the sides of the bowl. Using a spatula, fold the flour and salt into the mixture just until no streaks of flour remain. Stir in the remaining 200g of chocolate.

Pour the mix into the prepared baking tray, using a spatula to evenly distribute it and smooth out the surface. Bake until just set, about 25–30 minutes.

Remove from the oven and let the brownies cool completely. If you can wait, we recommend placing in the fridge overnight and cutting the next day to achieve a fudge-like consistency. If not, get stuck in and enjoy.

THE BEST OF BOTH WORLDS

Butcher & Catch is a seafood and steak restaurant using the very best locally reared meat and the most sustainable fish and seafood to bring you modern British cooking at its best.

In 2017, friends Liam Ridge and Adam Pearce decided to open a restaurant specialising in locally reared meats and seasonal British fish. Naturally, they named it Butcher & Catch to highlight the best of land and sea, with an emphasis on food that is accessible to anybody. Their aim was to create menus which are adventurous, focusing on typically underutilised cuts of meat and fish to introduce guests to dishes they might never have seen before.

"Locally sourced food and drink is the heart of the restaurant, and without such an amazing abundance of produce on our doorstep our vision wouldn't be possible. We have endless local suppliers, such as Hendersons Relish, Our Cow Molly, John Crawshaws Butchers, Aqua Garden Organics and many more. The Butcher & Catch team love the belly pork from Sheffield's own Moss Valley Fine Meats, while oysters sourced from family-run Lindisfarne Oysters based in Northumberland are a firm favourite with guests."

Menus are built around and inspired by the seasons, celebrating bright and vibrant flavours in the summer time, and warming, hearty, earthy flavours in winter months. You can see this approach the moment you walk into the restaurant, thanks to the open kitchen alongside a meat and fish counter that celebrates all of that day's produce in its glory. The entire building and decor is geared around this transparency and honesty, creating an atmosphere that's relaxed and inviting.

Butcher & Catch now also has a sister restaurant, Chop Shop Bar & Grill, which opened in 2022 and is situated in Kelham Island. Both venues follow the same ethos but differ in their offering and complement each other greatly. Butcher & Catch focuses on more complex flavour combinations, bringing several quality ingredients together including fish and seafood to create innovate dishes, whereas Chop Shop Bar & Grill puts the emphasis on unadulterated flavour from quality cuts of meat and open flame chargrill cooking to deliver steaks, chops, ribs and other cuts of meat in their purest form.

With a full calendar of events planned, from bottomless brunch to wine pairings to cocktail classes and monthly socials, Butcher & Catch are always looking for new opportunities and partnerships to bring their love of hospitality to a wider audience.

LINDISFARNE "FISH & CHIP" OYSTER

Preparation time: 30 minutes | Cooking time: 5 minutes | Serves 6

This recipe is one of the chefs' favourites, primarily because it encapsulates what Butcher & Catch is really about, which is taking fantastic British produce that people might not have tried before and making it accessible in a really fun and creative way. This dish is a play on traditional fish and chips, but uses a beautiful Lindisfarne oyster as its base, surrounded by flavours of a classic chippy.

For the beer battered oyster

6 Lindisfarne oysters (any variety will suffice)
300g self-raising flour
125ml chilled carbonated beer
125ml chilled soda water
10g sea salt
500ml rapeseed oil (any cooking oil will suffice)

For the straw potatoes

2 Maris Piper potatoes
5g sea salt

For the tartare sauce

20g gherkins, 20g capers
5g parsley
10g shallots
300g mayonnaise
15g Dijon mustard
5ml lemon juice, 10g harissa
5g each salt & pepper

For the vinegar gel

120g malt vinegar
2g Ultratex (thickening agent)

To serve

20g pea shoots
1 large lemon, cut into 6 wedges

For the beer battered oyster

Shuck the oysters and set to one side. Clean the oyster shell for serving in. Whisk 250g of the flour with the beer, soda water and salt until you have the consistency of thick cream. Heat the oil in a deep pan or deep fat fryer to 200°c. Coat the oyster meat in the remaining flour, then dip into the beer batter and mix well to coat. Drop the battered oysters into the hot oil one by one and cook for 90 seconds until golden brown. Remove and drain well, sprinkling with sea salt to finish.

For the straw potatoes

Cut the potatoes into thin matchsticks and drop into cold water for 10 minutes. Drain and pat until very dry. Place into the hot oil you used to fry the oysters and cook for 3 minutes until crispy and golden. Drain to remove excess oil and sprinkle with sea salt to taste. Leave to cool.

For the tartare sauce

Finely dice the gherkins, capers, parsley and shallots. Place them in a bowl and add the mayonnaise, Dijon mustard, lemon juice, harissa, salt, and pepper. Mix until everything is well incorporated.

For the vinegar gel

Whisk the malt vinegar and Ultratex (thickening agent) together until it forms a thick gel consistency. Place into squeezy bottle.

To serve

Place the straw potatoes on a plate, squeeze a couple dots of vinegar gel on top and then place the cleaned oyster shell on top of the straw potatoes. Place a tablespoon of tartare sauce inside the oyster shell. Place the cooked beer battered oyster on top of the tartare sauce. Dot with more vinegar gel. Top with a couple of pea shoots and place a wedge of lemon on the side. Enjoy.

REALIGNING YOUR CHAKRAS

With three sites in the UK, as well as a fourth in India, The Chakra Lounge offers irresistible Indian cuisine with a modern British twist.

Back in 2019, The Chakra Lounge became the first 'lounge café' in the heart of Derbyshire spa-town, Buxton. Since then, the Indo-Western café has gone from strength to strength opening its first Sheffield site, in Fitzalan Square, in October 2020.

The café prides itself on being 90% veggie and vegan, serving up a unique take on Indian and British cuisines from a quirky menu including breakfast items like 'Grandma's special turmeric porridge' and other twists on Western breakfasts only 'if Indians did them'.

Elsewhere on the menu are popular Indian snacks like maggi noodles and samosa chaat, heartier portions of curry and rice bowls, as well as authentic Indian coffee, and delicious cakes, many of which are vegan and gluten free.

Founder Sam moved to the UK from India in 2008 as a student. "When you come here from India, you have a culture shock. Trying to live on a budget as a student and trying to find things which are available in this country to mix with our own spices was difficult and is how the idea for The Chakra Lounge originally came about all those years ago.

"This is the food we've always wanted to do. It's the food that we had when we were kids and grew up eating. It's mother's cooking. It's not like what you get in other Indian restaurants. Even the coffee, which is Malabar, uses South Indian coffee beans. We're focused on getting things straight from India."

The Sheffield site is one of four The Chakra Lounge venues, with thriving ventures already established in Buxton, Bakewell, and India. Sam's younger brother was a chef in Hyatt until he moved to the UK in 2021 and has now taken over the 'cheffing side' of the business in Sheffield. Sam has been in the hospitality industry since 2006, when, after completing his masters in hospitality at the University of Derby, he opened his first restaurant, serving British cuisine.

It wasn't until Sam got into reiki and spiritualism that he opened the first Chakra Lounge. "The idea was to make an experience where people can come and relax, somewhere they're not on edge. It's not about being quick and high table turnover. It's a place where people can come and balance their thoughts and mind, and let their whole body relax.

"After Buxton, we always wanted to open in Sheffield and do something near the university, and this place felt right. The response has been great."

vibes

THE CHAKRA LOUNGE

THE CHAKRA LOUNGE
CLOSED
SUMMER SPECIALS
COCOBERRY SMOOTHIE
Watermelon Shikanji
ICED DIRTY CHAI
Mango Mastani
VEGAN CURRY BOX
BE LOCAL

PALAK PANEER

Preparation time: 5 minutes | Cooking time: 15 minutes | Serves 4

I'm from a Punjabi family so my mother regularly made palak paneer when I was growing up. It was also a fixture of celebratory meals and occasions, and we'd serve it whenever family came to visit – it's very special for us Punjabi. I like my mother's version the best because it's so simple.

3 tbsp clarified butter
5 bay leaves
½ tbsp cumin
3-4 black cardamom
3 cinnamon sticks
5 cloves
2 onions, finely chopped
4-5 tomatoes, chopped
2 tbsp garlic and ginger paste
Salt, to taste
¼ tbsp black pepper
1 tbsp garam masala
½ tbsp fenugreek
250g cottage cheese
500g spinach leaves, puréed
2 tbsp coconut cream

In a pan warm the clarified butter over a low heat. Add the bay leaves, cumin, black cardamom, cinnamon sticks, and cloves and cook them for a few seconds in the butter. Next, add the chopped onions and let them sweat, then add in the tomatoes. Mix in the garlic and ginger paste and allow it to cook through for a few minutes. Make sure to add a little water, if necessary, to ensure the contents don't burn. Now it's time to add in the powdered spices – salt, black pepper, garam masala and fenugreek powder – and let them cook for a few seconds on a high heat.

Cut the cottage cheese into cubes, add it to the pan, and toss it with all the spices and garam masala. After that, add in the spinach purée and cook on a high heat for a few seconds. Finally, finish it off with the coconut cream. Check the saltiness and adjust according to taste.

Enjoy!

GET YOUR TASTEBUDS TINGLING!

With a restaurant on The Moor and a new street food stand in Cutlery Works, China Red is the place to go for authentic Szechuan food in Sheffield.

Established in 2006, China Red strives to offer authentic Szechuan cuisine in the heart of the city. Traditionally trained chefs turn fresh ingredients into specialty dishes that rival those offered in China. The atmospheric restaurant offers ample seating to accommodate anyone from couples to large parties, and the upper floor also boasts a karaoke bar with state-of-the-art amenities and equipment. Kelvin Quick, who also runs the successful ALS Gongcha bubble tea venture in Sheffield, is the current owner of China Red, having worked his way up from a part-time position back in 2008, and is passionate about the restaurant's commitment to deliciously different dishes.

Szechuan food, originating from Sichuan Province in Southwest China, uses spices for flavour rather than intense heat and often includes Szechuan peppercorns, an ingredient unlike any other that creates a tingling sensation on your tongue when eaten. Unlike most of the Chinese restaurants and takeaways we are used to in the UK, China Red focuses specifically on this unique cuisine and serves authentic dishes such as hot pot (a simmering broth filled with various tasty ingredients like egg noodles, eggs, meats, veggies, tofu and even dumplings) and lamb with cumin.

The restaurant makes its own pickled vegetables, a staple in typical Szechuan households, and chilli oil, which Kelvin describes as "the essence of Szechuan food" and fills the restaurant with the aroma of slow roasted chillies and spices as it's being freshly made each week. Alongside Chinese groceries, the restaurant sources fresh produce like meat and seafood from local suppliers in Sheffield. This approach means they often have new specials available, alongside a flexible menu which encourages diners to share dishes so everyone can try a bit of everything.

All China Red's chefs are from Sichuan Province, creating a strong identity and ensuring authentic cookery at both the restaurant and street food stall. There are some classic Chinese dishes available alongside the more adventurous options, so whether you are completely new to Szechuan food or addicted to the tongue-tingling flavours of this delicious cuisine, China Red is not to be missed.

CHINA RED
RESTAURANT
満庭紅
CHINA RED RESTAURANT
満庭紅
川菜館
正宗川菜 名厨主理
from £10.50

POACHED BEEF IN HOT CHILLI OIL

Preparation time: 25 minutes | Cooking time: 25 minutes | Serves 4-6

This dish originated from the Northern Song Dynasty of China and dates back at least a thousand years. Tender beef slices are cooked in a classic Sichuan style called shuizhu which means 'water boiled' and chilli oils made with a variety of spices and peppers add the finishing touch.

300g sliced beef (tenderloin is best)
2 tbsp Chinese rice wine
1½ tbsp corn starch
1 tbsp soy sauce
1½ tsp sesame oil
1½ tsp salt
1 egg white
80g Chinese leaves
1 spring onion
½ a leek
35g vegetable oil
5g dried chillies
5g Sichuan peppercorn
1 stick of cinnamon bark
4 bay leaves
2 star anise
80g beansprouts
5 slices of garlic
4 slices of fresh ginger
3 tbsp chilli bean paste
3g chilli powder
500ml chicken or pork bone stock (can be replaced by water)
5g minced garlic
3-4 sprigs of fresh coriander

Firstly, put the beef slices in a bowl with 1 tablespoon of the Chinese rice wine, the corn starch, soy sauce, sesame oil, salt, egg white and 3 tablespoons of water. Stir everything together until all the beef slices are coated and then marinate for 20 minutes. Meanwhile, cut the Chinese leaves into 5cm lengths, and cut the spring onion and leek into 3cm lengths.

Next, fry the spicy toppings. Heat up a wok to 100°c and pour in 30g of the vegetable oil. Stir fry the dried chillies and Sichuan peppercorns for about 1 minute, then remove them but leave the oil. Finely chop the dried chillies and peppercorns. In the same pan and oil, deep fry the spring onion, leek, cinnamon bark, bay leaf and anise until they turn golden brown. Remove those ingredients from the oil and keep the oil in a bowl for later.

Boil the Chinese leaves and beansprouts in a large saucepan of water with half a teaspoon of salt and 2 drops of oil until lightly wilted, about 5 minutes. Transfer the vegetables to a large plate and discard the water.

Start to prepare the broth in the wok by stir frying the sliced garlic and ginger with the chilli bean paste and chilli powder until fragrant. Pour in the stock or water and bring to the boil, which should take about 5 minutes, then add the marinated beef slices piece by piece until they are fully cooked. This should take about 10 minutes. Pour everything from the saucepan onto the large plate with the cooked Chinese leaves and beansprouts.

Finally, start sizzling and garnishing. Scatter the minced garlic and chopped chillies and peppercorns over the cooked beef and vegetables. Heat up a pan and pour in the reserved spiced oil. When the oil starts smoking, pour it carefully and evenly over the garlic, chilli and peppercorn topping. Lastly, garnish the dish with fresh coriander and serve.

GONG-PO CHICKEN

Preparation time: 15 minutes | Cooking time: 10 minutes | Serves 2-4

This well-known Chinese recipe was one of the Qing Dynasty's imperial dishes and is a classic from Guizhou and Sichuan. The characteristics of gong-po chicken are sweet and spicy but not fierce; tender chicken combines with the crunchy peanuts and cucumber for a delicious flavour and texture.

200g chicken breast
2 tbsp soy sauce
1 tbsp Chinese rice wine
1 tsp white pepper
½ tsp salt
15g cornflour
10g vegetable oil
1/3 of a cucumber
2 spring onions
1 tbsp bean paste
1 tbsp mature vinegar
1 tsp hoisin sauce
½ tsp chicken powder
½ tsp white sugar
10g garlic slices
5g dried chillies
3g minced ginger
3g Sichuan peppercorns
50g fried peanuts
3g chopped green onion
1g white sesame seeds

First, beat the chicken breast with the back of a knife to tenderise the meat and then cut into small pieces about the size of a thumbnail. In a bowl, combine 1 tablespoon of the soy sauce with the Chinese rice wine, white pepper, salt, 10g of the cornflour and 5g of the vegetable oil. Whisk until smooth, then add the chicken to the bowl and toss to coat. Marinate for 10 minutes.

Next, dice the cucumber and spring onion for later. Making the sauce in a small bowl by whisking the remaining soy sauce and cornflour with the bean paste, mature vinegar, hoisin sauce, chicken powder and white sugar until evenly combined.

Pour the remaining vegetable oil into a large pan over a medium-high heat (about 70°c) and let it heat up for 30 seconds before adding the marinated chicken. Stir fry until the chicken is golden and almost cooked through, about 8 minutes. Remove the pan from the heat, transfer the chicken to a bowl and set aside.

Reheat the same pan with more oil if necessary for about 30 seconds, then add the garlic slices, dried chillies, minced ginger and Sichuan peppercorn. Fry until fragrant, then return the chicken to the pan and pour in the prepared sauce. Stir fry evenly over a high heat until the sauce has reduced and been absorbed into the meat, about 5 minutes.

To finish, add the diced cucumber and spring onion to the pan, stir fry everything together for 1 minute, then turn off the heat. Stir in the peanuts and mix it all together. Transfer the dish to a beautiful plate, then garnish with the chopped green onion and white sesame seeds. Serve immediately.

HIGH STEAKS FOR MEAT LOVERS

Chop Shop Bar & Grill celebrates all things meat, using the very best local produce and wood-fired cooking to enhance the natural flavours of chops, steaks, rotisserie chicken and more.

Following on from the success of Butcher & Catch, which opened in 2017, business partners Liam and Adam decided to opened Chop Shop Bar & Grill in Kelham Island in 2022. The concept was to create a space where the focus was on unadulterated cuts of meat, cooked simply and traditionally over wood fires: the ultimate steak and chop house. They also wanted a space that could deliver a huge range of fantastic beers and wines with scope for larger hospitality events.

The majority of the Chop Shop menu is cooked over wood fires on their traditional Argentinian Asado grill. This cooking method, paired with the very best locally reared meats, delivers an unforgettable flavour which has always been at the heart of great meat cookery. They have a very relaxed environment with emphasis on the social aspect of the dining experience, so much of the menu is geared towards sharing and grazing. This is paired with a fantastic bar area serving a range of wine, beer and cocktails for the perfect evening out.

Locally reared and sourced meats are the star of the show at Chop Shop, which was rather fittingly named after the original steak section of the Butcher & Catch menu. Like its older sister, the restaurant is open plan, creating drinking and dining experiences that perfectly complement each other. The aromas of the food cooking capture the attention of everyone who visits, especially the unmistakable scent of barbecues when the Asado grill is in full swing, and the chickens slowly roasting in the rotisserie oven – a customer favourite – are on display for all to see.

The chefs are inspired to bring out the very best flavour possible from whatever cut of meat they are cooking. It's about giving the cheapest cuts of meats the attention they deserve, enhancing the natural flavours with subtle yet effective ingredients and cooking methods, and most importantly staying true to yourself when it comes to sourcing the best from the abundance of amazing local meat producers on our doorstep in Sheffield. A firm favourite with the staff is the amazingly tender slow-cooked BBQ baby back pork ribs, cooked in a Henderson's Relish barbecue sauce and perfectly accompanied by chorizo mac 'n' cheese. Both the ribs and chorizo are from local farmers Moss Valley Fine Meats who have been supplying award-winning pork to both restaurants since day one.

CHOP
SHOP

EST.2022
CHOP
SHOP
BAR & GRILL

HENDERSON'S
RELISH

EST.2022
CHOP

EST.2022
CHOP
SHOP
BAR & GRILL

EST.2022
CHOP
SHOP
BAR & GRILL

MOSS VALLEY BBQ BABY BACK RIBS & JALAPEÑO CHEDDAR CORNBREAD

Preparation time: 1 hour | Cooking time: 3 hours | Serves 4

This is a recipe that sums up Chop Shop Bar & Grill perfectly. No nonsense, bold flavours, celebrating local produce and enhancing the flavour of the meat. We use local Moss Valley pork ribs for this recipe, and Sheffield's own Henderson's Relish to make a barbecue sauce that perfectly complements the meat, resulting in these sweet, sticky, tangy, melt in the mouth baby back ribs.

For the pork spice rub

50g each brown sugar, ground cumin and Chinese five spice

25g each salt, garlic powder, mustard powder, ground black pepper, cayenne pepper and smoked paprika

For the Henderson's BBQ sauce

300ml tomato ketchup

100ml Henderson's Relish

50ml each bourbon whisky and black treacle, 75g brown sugar

5g each smoked paprika & chilli powder

For the baby back ribs

4 racks of baby back ribs

200g pork spice rub

500ml Henderson's BBQ sauce

400ml apple juice

200ml Henderson's Relish

For the jalapeño cheddar cornbread

950ml buttermilk

550g polenta or cornmeal

500g self-raising flour, 450g melted butter

250g grated cheddar cheese

200g sweetcorn, pulsed

150g tinned jalapeños, chopped

50g sugar, 8 eggs

10g each baking powder and salt

For the pork spice rub

Combine all of the ingredients until thoroughly mixed. Store in an airtight container.

For the Henderson's BBQ sauce

Simmer all the ingredients together in a deep pan until thick, smooth and well incorporated. Leave to cool before bottling.

For the baby back ribs

Rub the ribs with the pork spice rub until well coated, then leave to marinate for at least 1 hour (up to 24 hours is fine). Seal the ribs on a hot flat griddle or barbecue until each side is lightly browned, then transfer them to a deep roasting tin. In a bowl, whisk all the wet ingredients together (reserving 100ml of the BBQ sauce for glazing at the end) and pour half this mixture over the ribs. Cover with parchment paper and then seal the tin with tin foil or a lid. Cook in the oven at 150°c for 90 minutes. Remove from the oven, turn the ribs over and cover with the remaining wet mixture. Cook for a further 90 minutes at the same temperature.

For the jalapeño cheddar cornbread

Mix all the ingredients together (in a stand mixer if possible) until they are the consistency of muffin batter. Spoon into non-stick muffin tins and bake at 200°c for 12-14 minutes.

To serve

Carefully place the ribs onto a plate and drizzle with the remaining BBQ sauce. Serve the warm jalapeño cheddar cornbread on the side. Use your fingers to get stuck in and enjoy.

TAKE ME TO CHURCH

Housed in Kelham Island's listed Osborn Works, Church lives up to its full name as a 'temple of fun' with the eclectic combination of indulgent vegan food, drinks and retro arcade vibes.

The concept of Sheffield's first arcade bar was developed by Bring Me The Horizon frontman Oliver Sykes, a longtime vegan who wanted to create a place that served vegan food for everyone. Inspired by the unusual spaces and religious iconography he saw on a trip to South America, Oli chose Osborn Works in Kelham Island to bring his vision to life. As the only industrial building designed by famed Victorian architect William John Hale, who was responsible for some of the areas more iconic churches, it was fitting that on the eve of the building's 100th anniversary in 2018, Osborn Works was reborn as Church – Temple of Fun.

Church has a 100% vegan bar and restaurant, designed to satisfy the taste buds of vegans and omnivores alike. The menu is mostly comfort food – including big burgers, kebabs and chicken tenders made in-house to the kitchen's own recipe – but they are branching out into healthier options too, such as the 'Build your own Buddha bowl' which offers hundreds if not thousands of combinations of ingredients! Church also does a completely vegan Sunday Dinner starring a Beyond Meat wellington, seasonal veg and homemade Hendo's gravy of course. Oli and his team want to prove that vegan food can be exciting, innovative and above all, delicious.

This aim is reflected in the bar menus too, which include a broad spectrum of both alcoholic and non-alcoholic options to cater for all needs and tastes. The cocktails are a signature feature, with a staple selection completed by seasonal creations, alongside their new CBD offerings. Drinks can be enjoyed inside or outside on the balcony terrace overlooking the River Don, or you can lose yourself over games with the cosy Playstation pods, a pool table and retro arcade machines.

Church is also a live music venue and regularly hosts free movie nights which sometimes feature themed food and drink, as well as decor to really transport you into the film. The mezzanine space above the main floor is perfect if you have a large group celebrating a special occasion. Saturdays are always buzzing with people coming in for the drinks and DJs, while weekday evenings are ideal for a chilled dining experience. The warm and friendly atmosphere creates a welcoming space, with customers often praising how lovely the staff are. Church is all about being open to everyone and, whether you're vegan or not, serving up the best vegan food and drink you've ever had!

VEGAN MAC 'N' CHEESE

Preparation time: 45 minutes | Cooking time: 15 minutes | Serves 4

Vegan cheese gets a bit of a bad rep, so we wanted to showcase our homemade recipe from Cam and Aimee, our amazing kitchen team. It has a bit of a twist, plus it's so creamy and cheesy you won't even know it's vegan.

50g butter
50g flour
500ml soy milk
½ tbsp dill
½ tbsp parsley
½ tbsp paprika
½ tbsp salt
½ tbsp black pepper
250g grated cheese (we recommend Violife)
240ml vegan cream
500g macaroni pasta
120g vegan bacon, diced (we recommend THIS™)
100g gherkins, diced
150g panko breadcrumbs

Melt the butter in a pan over a medium heat, add the flour and whisk to make a roux. Cook for 30 seconds to 1 minute, then start to add the soy milk little by little while whisking to prevent lumps. Once all the soy milk is incorporated, bring the sauce to a simmer while constantly mixing to prevent the sauce from burning.

Once the sauce starts to bubble, remove it from the heat, pour into a flat dish and allow to cool to room temperature.

Add the herbs, spices, salt, pepper, grated cheese, and cream to the cooled sauce and stir to combine.

TIP: It's very important that the sauce has cooled before you add the cheese. If it's melted into the sauce before cooling, it'll solidify and separate when warming up.

Fill a saucepan with salted boiling water and cook the macaroni for around 7-9 minutes. Once cooked, drain and place to one side.

In another saucepan, combine the cheese sauce with the diced bacon and gherkins. Heat gently and stir until the grated cheese has melted into the sauce.

Add the macaroni to the sauce and continue to stir until the pasta is hot.

To serve

Transfer the mixture to an ovenproof dish (you can use one large dish, or individual ones) and then top with the panko breadcrumbs. Lightly toast under the grill until golden. This is great accompanied by garlic bread, or a salad.

HAVANA GREAT TIME

For 22 years, Cubana has been bringing a vibrant selection of Latino vibes to Sheffield through live music, award-winning tapas and a truly enviable rum selection.

Now nothing short of a Steel City culinary institution, what today encompasses two bustling floors of dancing, drinks and tapas started life in relatively humble fashion as a cosy backstreet hangout on Trippet Lane. Adrian Bagnoli opened the first Cubana with business partner Brad Charlesworth in November 2000, the first tapas bar of its kind in Sheffield, which achieved huge acclaim before moving to their hugely popular Leopold Square venue in 2014.

An authentic atmosphere is at the heart of all things Cubana; the walls are adorned with Havana-inspired murals, live music plays every night of the week, and an extensive menu combines classic Spanish tapas with South American flair and flavour, including a welcome selection of both meat and plant-based options. The set menus are particularly popular when it comes to celebrating an occasion, serving up veritable banquets of tapas to hungry customers looking for a variety of expertly prepared dishes.

While the cocktails and wines on offer are mouth-wateringly good, the rum menu is quite simply "one of the best in the world" as described by acclaimed rum connoisseur, global rum ambassador Ian. A. V. Burrell. Their latest collection, which was four years in the making, brings together an incredible 305 varieties of rum – the main event being one of the rarest bottles you can get your hands on, 'The Havana Club 1519', and retails at a rather pricey £250 per shot (though there are many much more affordable options available!).

Over the years Adrian and Brad's small slice of Havana has welcomed some esteemed guests through its doors, including famed Panamanian boxer Roberto Duran and the legendary Buena Vista Social Club. However, the ultimate seal of approval came in 2014 when Dr Aleida Guevara, daughter of famous Cuban revolutionary Che Guevara, visited for a memorable dinner and posed for a picture beneath a portrait of her father that has decorated the Cubana walls since its opening.

Moving forward, Adrian tells us we can expect more of the same from a venue that for over two decades has set the bar for sumptuous Latino flavours and an immersive, welcoming atmosphere. "We've enjoyed over 22 years of providing the people of Sheffield with the full Cubana experience: exotic cocktails, friendly customer service, brilliant live music, and of course, stunning tapas made with love by our experienced kitchen team – all under the one roof. We're proud to be a longstanding part of the city's food and drink scene, so here's to another 20-plus years of keeping the party going! Salud!"

CUBANA
TAPAS RESTAURANT
CUBAN BAR
WAZWĀN

EMPANADA DE RES Y CORDERO

Preparation time: 1 hour | Cooking time: 30 minutes | Serves 4

An Argentinian favourite: empanada pastry filled with minced beef and lamb, tomato and onions, seasoned with cumin, coriander and black pepper.

For the dough
500g plain flour
250ml water
90ml vegetable oil
7g salt
1 egg, beaten

For the filling
1 medium onion
1 clove of garlic
250g lamb mince
250g beef mince
2 tbsp tomato purée
2 tbsp chopped fresh coriander
1 tbsp smoked paprika
1 tbsp ground cumin

Place all the ingredients for the dough except the egg into a bowl and knead until it comes together. Let the dough rest for 30 minutes.

While the dough is resting, peel and dice the onion and garlic, then fry with a little oil until softened. Add both the mince meats and fry until cooked through, then add the tomato purée, fresh coriander, smoked paprika, and ground cumin. Season with salt and pepper to taste.

Let the mince mixture cook for about 5 more minutes, then set aside to cool. Meanwhile, roll out your chilled dough to about 4mm thick.

Use a pastry cutter or a plate to cut out a circle. Spoon the cooled mince mixture into the centre of the circle. Brush the edges with the beaten egg, then fold the dough over to create a semicircle and crimp around the edges with a fork to seal the filling in. Repeat with the remaining dough and filling.

Bake the empanadas on a tray in a preheated oven at 180°c for 15-20 minutes. Alternatively, you can deep fry them in oil at 180°c until golden brown.

DOMO'S WHERE THE HEART IS

Found on the ground floor of the heritage-listed Eagle Works building in bustling Kelham Island, Domo brings a sparkling slice of Sardinian life to Sheffield.

Since opening in the summer of 2019, Domo restaurant has proved immensely popular, bringing traditional Sardinian coastal flavours to eager Sheffield plates.

Domo co-owner Raffaelle Busceddu hails from Castelsardo, a small Sardinian port town, and the restaurant is built in the image of his idyllic hometown, with a sunbathed courtyard, perfect for alfresco drinking and dining. Inside, you'll find a stunning and spacious restaurant and bar area adorned with Sardinian masks, handwoven baskets and Mediterranean-style plants.

Raffa, who also co-owns a restaurant with his uncle in Castelsardo, along with his partner Sarah Elliot have years of experience in the restaurant business bewtween them and decided to put that knowledge and skill to good use by launching their own venue. Once the doors to Domo swung open, the family converged on Sheffield to help run the place and install some truly authentic Italian character to the eatery.

Even before tucking into the food from one of Domo's inspired menus, it hits just how impressive a place it is. There's the hustle and bustle of a family-run kitchen in one corner – frenetic, passionate and fervent. It's quite something to see that manifest into a plate of hearty food, served with a smile and a ''buon appetito'', of course.

The word Domo means home, and it's clear to see that Sarah and Raffa have brought their version of home to the city of Sheffield, with that unique blend of incredible home cooked-style food served up in an atmosphere akin to a family meal at nonna's place.

If the traditional and welcoming feel is the entrée, then the extensive menu at Domo is – quite literally - the pièce de résistance. The menu is comprehensive and reflects the wide-ranging flavours enjoyed in authentic Sardinian cuisine. Divided into two sections, 'from the land' and 'from the sea', you can see the importance of sticking to tradition with key influences taken from a number of the region's areas.

Sarah and Rafaelle's own words sum up this gorgeous restaurant perfectly. "We pride ourselves on serving up food, drink and hospitality you would find in our small town of Castelsardo, Sardinia. We want you to experience the real Sardinian way of life. Whether you need coffee on the go, lunch with colleagues, after work drinks, feasts with the family, or cocktails at the weekend we serve up Sardinian tradition all day long. In Castelsardo our door is always open when there's food on the table. We welcome you to our restaurant like we would our home."

DOMO
DOMO

DOMO

APEROL
SPRITZ
CINZANO

CULURGIONES CON CREMA DI PECORINO E TARTUFO

Preparation time: 1 hour | Cooking time: 10 minutes | Makes around 40

Culurgiones is a traditional dish of stuffed pasta pockets from Ogliastra, a region in Sardinia. The filling is commonly made with boiled potatoes, olive oil, pecorino cheese, garlic, mint and nutmeg. We use our traditional family recipe from my uncle's famous Rocca ja restaurant in my home town of Castelsardo.

For the filling

3 large red potatoes
120g hard pecorino cheese
120g fresh pecorino cheese
10 fresh mint leaves, finely chopped

For the dough

600g re-milled semolina or durum wheat flour
300ml water at room temperature
Salt, to taste

For the sauce

Pecorino cream (can be bought in jars)
Truffle sauce
Pea shoots, to garnish

For the filling

Place the potatoes in a pan with cold water and bring to the boil. Cook the whole, unpeeled potatoes in salted water until fork tender – pierce them to check. Run them under cold water to cool, then peel and mash them. Grate the cheeses, then add them to the mash with the mint. Mix well, then cover the mixture with cling film and let it rest in the fridge for at least a couple of hours.

For the dough

Dissolve the salt in the water, then gradually add the salty water to the flour and knead continuously. Work energetically until a smooth and lump-free dough is obtained. Wrap the dough in cling film and let it rest for half an hour.

To make the culurgiones

Roll out the dough on a well-floured surface until you have thin sheets of about 1mm. Using a pastry cutter or a glass, cut out discs about 8cm (3 inches) in diameter. Place a portion of filling the size of a walnut on each disc. Close with the classic spike closure (YouTube it!) by pinching the ends and folding the dough onto itself until you close the culurgione. Place them on a floured tray.

To cook and serve

Cook the culurgiones in plenty of salted water for about 4-5 minutes, or 2 minutes from the moment they start floating. Put the pecorino cream in a pan with a spoonful of truffle sauce, then add a spoon of the culurgiones cooking water and let the sauce become smooth.

Transfer the culurgiones to the sauce with a slotted spoon and mix everything together. Serve on a rectangular plate, garnished with pea shoots.

RE-DOUGH-FINING COOKIES

A sister (or perhaps brother?) company to Bullion Chocolate, Doughboy takes pride in keeping a stream of gourmet treats coming for sweet-toothed Sheffielders.

Doughboy was born out of an idea to create a wholesale bakery for Bullion owner Max Scotford to stock their café and other local businesses with a selection of mouthwatering bakes. But as plans progressed, it didn't take long for the brand to uncover a separate life as a unique cookie takeout joint.

It's certainly a tasty concept: six oven-fresh cookies on the counter at any time, five of which rotate on a weekly basis, with a promise that you'll never see a certain flavour repeated in the same month. The only mainstay of the selection is the classic milk chocolate chip (no need to mess with perfection, right?) and you can also grab succulent brownies, chocolate bars, chilled milkshakes and delicious ice cream from local legends Our Cow Molly.

Flavour-wise, there really is something for everyone. Max tells us that if it tastes sweet, then you can make it into a cookie – and they've certainly proven that hypothesis by knocking up carrot cake, Bakewell Tart and even pina colada-inspired creations! A key inspiration was recreating the bright, family-friendly atmosphere of 1930s LA sweet shops, which you can see reflected in the vintage-style branding and bustling neighbourhood feel of the shop.

"We've had a great response since Doughboy opened its doors to walk-in customers," says Max. "We wanted a space where kids, adults and families could come and enjoy some lovingly made bakes. The constantly changing selection ensures there's something for everyone's taste, and we have plenty of vegan options available, too."

The premises are based at Aberdeen Court, just off Division Street, and Doughboy began life by supplying their good friends Steam Yard (situated next door) and Corner Store on Sharrow Vale Road with freshly baked goods. That client list has since grown to supply some of the region's most recognisable institutions: Chatsworth House, Sheffield Wednesday FC and Sheffield Hallam University all regularly stock a selection of indulgent bakes.

All cookies are baked, topped and finished on-site, and whether you're taking goodies home or perching on a seat outside to relax in their picturesque yard space, the goal remains the same: bringing the warmth and excitement back into enjoying sweet treats. Next time you're in town and the sugar cravings kick in, be sure to stop by and enjoy some truly top-tier bakes.

Doughboy
COOKIE SHOP
Doughboy

Doughboy

Doughboy
COOKIES & CREAM
COMBO
£4.99

DOUGHBOY CHOCOLATE CHIP COOKIES

Preparation time: 10-15 minutes | Cooking time: 10-12 minutes | Makes 10

Learn how to make our famous thick-cut, American-style, vegan cookies with this easy recipe.

128g margarine
209g sugar
¼ tsp vanilla
23g oat milk
260g plain flour
½ tsp baking powder
½ tsp bicarbonate of soda
½ tsp salt
140g dark chocolate chips

Preheat a fan oven to 160°c. Beat the margarine, sugar and vanilla together in a stand mixer until smooth and combined.

Add the oat milk and mix together, scrape down the bowl with a spatula and ensure everything is combined before proceeding. In a separate bowl, mix the dry ingredients together.

Add the dry flour mixture to the margarine mixture in two additions and beat until combined. Slowly mix in the chocolate to create an even spread through the whole batter.

Tip the dough out onto a work surface and portion into 10 evenly sized cookie pucks. Put the pucks on greaseproof paper and place on a baking tray.

Bake the cookies in the preheated oven for 10-12 minutes. The cookies are done when they look golden on the edges and have a gooey centre. Let the cookies cool off and then enjoy!

Doughboy

DYSHING UP GREAT FOOD AND DRINK

This independent café on Ecclesall Road serves all day breakfast, lunch, afternoon tea and Sunday lunch, all made in-house to be enjoyed alongside great coffee and a warm welcome.

Alice Cassinelli opened Dysh just after lockdown in 2021, beginning as a takeaway only due to restrictions. She had aspired to be a café owner from a very young age and spent a lot of time training as a chef in various restaurants to gain the skills and experience that make Dysh what it is today. Stuart Broomhead, Alice's fiancé, heads up the front of house team and the pair have a passion for the hospitality industry that shines through at the café. They aim to work with likeminded people to create a special place for all customers to feel relaxed and looked after.

A cornerstone of this approach is the inclusive menu at Dysh, which Alice and her team spend a lot of time developing to suit as many dietary requirements as possible, including plenty of gluten-free and vegan options. The offering changes twice a year, inspired by Alice's knowledge of fine dining techniques which she transforms into wholesome food that people can enjoy in a casual and affordable setting. "I like to create dishes based around people's childhood favourites that bring a sort of nostalgia," Alice explains.

Fresh ingredients, seasonal produce and local suppliers are also key to the food and drink at Dysh. Alice and Stuart like to work with friendly and ethical companies wherever possible, from Moss Valley Fine Meats to Cafeology, one of the city's most sustainable independent coffee suppliers. They also champion some of Sheffield's talented residents through a minimalist approach to the décor at Dysh, creating a "blank canvas" to showcase artwork by Luke Horton and handmade crafts from the Work Ltd social enterprise on Ringinglow Road.

This commitment to celebrating the city has taken Dysh from strength to strength since their challenging beginnings. "We have been very lucky to be able to employ an amazing team of talented and experienced people, many of whom worked in big roles around Sheffield and have come to us due to our passionate outlook and our sociable work environment," says Alice. The chef also credits her family for their ongoing support, the fantastic lecturers at Sheffield College where she began training, working alongside Nathan Smith at The Old Vicarage, and her year at the Michelin-starred L'Enclume in Cumbria. With such a wealth of hospitality expertise and a genuine warmth behind the venture, it's no surprise that Dysh is already a fixture of Sheffield's daytime dining scene.

Dysh
COFFEE & KITCHEN

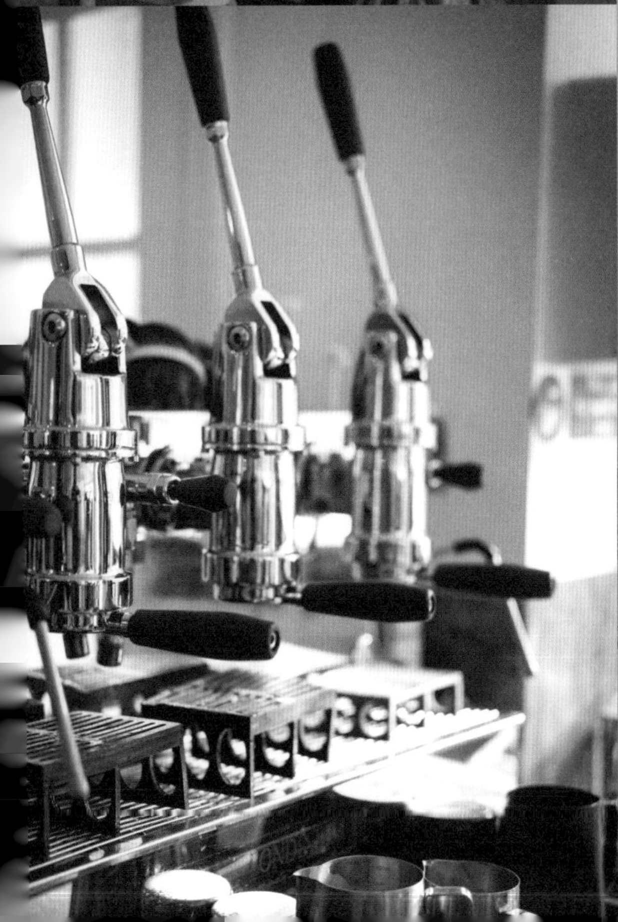

CUPPA?
REST YA LEGS
mek ya sen at ome

PISTACHIO AND CHERRY BAKEWELL TART

Preparation time: 45 minutes | Cooking time: 25 minutes | Serves 10

We run weekend specials throughout the year - our most popular specials then make it onto our menu which we make seasonal changes to. This dish was so popular it just had to come on to our menu due to people power!

For the pastry

300g gluten-free flour (we use Dove's Farm)

50g icing sugar

½ tsp xanthan gum

Pinch of salt

100g baking butter

1 egg + 1 egg yolk

For the cherry jam

500g frozen cherries

100g caster sugar

For the pistachio frangipane filling

125g baking butter

125g caster sugar

1 medium egg

1 tsp gluten-free flour

125g pistachios, finely chopped or blitzed

Method

Begin by making the pastry. Combine the dry ingredients and then rub in the butter. Once the mixture is at breadcrumb stage, add the egg and egg yolk until combined. Do not over mix. Wrap the pastry in cling film and leave to rest in the fridge.

While this is resting, make the cherry jam. Combine the cherries and caster sugar in a bowl, cover tightly with cling film, then place over a pan of boiling water and leave until the sugar has dissolved.

Return to the pastry. Roll the chilled pastry out on a floured surface until it is the thickness of a pound coin. Use this to line a 10-inch fluted tart tin and bake at 180°c for 25 minutes.

To make the frangipane, whip the butter and sugar together in a stand mixer (or use a handheld whisk) until very pale, almost white in colour. Now add the egg and beat on high speed. Once the egg is incorporated, stop the mixer and fold in the dry ingredients.

Now to assemble the tart. Take the baked pastry case and pour in the cherry jam, using a palette knife or the back of a spoon to level it and coat the base. Now spoon in the frangipane mix and smooth out. Ensure all the jam is covered with the pistachio mixture.

Place the Bakewell tart in a preheated oven at 160°c for 20-25 minutes, then cool and slice to serve.

A UNIQUE BLEND

Using a handmade roaster crafted from the finest Sheffield steel, Frazer's Coffee ethically source beans from across the globe and create exciting blends to share with the people of the city.

Frazer Habershon's passion for coffee started at home. When it came to brewing up, his mum would always ensure there were good quality beans available in the house. It would stand him in good stead years later, as the local lad embarked on a journey from avid coffee drinker to building one of the city's best-known coffee brands, powered in true 'made in Sheffield' style by a state-of-the-art roaster made from Forgemasters steel.

Prior to the first lockdown in 2020, Frazer's Coffee had become a well-established wholesale business, selling their coffee to a wide range of cafes, shops, delis and local businesses while flying the flag for direct trade, building stronger connections with farmers across the globe, and ensuring the stories behind each bean were told. However, when the pandemic hit and multiple stockists across the region were quickly closed, the roastery was forced to temporarily cease trading as an uncertain future beckoned.

"It was a difficult period and worrying time for any business," says Frazer. "But I was really moved when my inbox became inundated with retail orders from customers at home. The penny quickly dropped: we distributed to over 80 wholesale businesses, which is a lot of people drinking our coffee, and during the lockdown, people wanted to continue doing just that. We pivoted to becoming an online retail business, delivering directly to customers and offering collections at the roastery. It allowed us to come out of the other side stronger, setting a lot of the groundwork for what was to come."

Now split evenly across wholesale and retail, Frazer's next big step as a business came in March of this year, when they opened their first coffee shop at Kommune Food Hall. Frazer's Coffee Emporium offers a tailored service where you can buy your beans and brewing equipment while learning directly from staff about the different methods of making coffee from home. The welcoming café space also offers a full breakfast and brunch menu, fresh pizzas, treats from local bakeries – and, of course, a full coffee menu including their famous nitro cold brew (now available in 330ml cans from their website).

Today Frazer's sends their award-winning blends all over the country, but the key ethos remains the same: providing high-quality, ethically sourced coffee at honest prices while teaching anyone interested how to get the most out of every cup.

Frazer's

Olam
Specialty
Coffee
Arabica Coffee
Natural
El Volcan and El Pelon
Jinotega Region

Dose
Yield
Time
Brew Ratio:
MENU
coffee

HOW TO BREW PROPER COFFEE -ESPRESSO

Brewing coffee is like baking; you need to follow a recipe to achieve consistent results. We teach cafés and coffee shops a simple but effective recipe to follow based on the dose, yield and time. These three things allow you to repeat flavours and extraction but can be applied to any brewing method. Over the next few pages, we are going to explain three methods that you can try at home: espresso, filter and cafetiere.

Espresso
Dose = 18g   Time = 27-32 seconds   Yield = 45ml

Top Tip:
The grinder controls the time this method takes, so the finer the grind, the longer the espresso will be. Ground coffee should feel like super fine, almost like gritty flour.

We use the Full Monty espresso blend for this recipe. Working with a traditional espresso machine can be intimidating and also not very forgiving, but if you follow these three simple steps it will make your coffee really stand out.

Dose
This means how much coffee you put in the group handle of the machine before tamping.

Time
This is as simple as starting a stopwatch when you press your brew and stopping it when the brew has finished. Be warned, this is the hard part!

Yield
This means how much espresso comes out. Use weighing scales to get an accurate result and remember that for coffee, millilitres weigh the same as grams so if your scales say 45g this means you have 45ml of espresso.

Brewing Goals
The aim is to have all three variables (dose, time and yield) in line with the recipe above. The dose and yield can be controlled by simply weighing the coffee accurately, but the hard part is controlling how long the process takes because this is determined by the grind of the coffee. The rule here is the finer the grind, the longer the shot will last, and vice versa: the coarser the grind, the quicker the shot.

Once this method has been practiced, it can open up a huge variety of coffees because it is the foundation of any modern espresso-based drink. My personal favourite is a flat white, which is made by steaming 200ml of whole milk to 60°c with a small amount of foam to be served as a 6oz drink.

HOW TO BREW PROPER COFFEE -FILTER COFFEE

Filter coffee comes in different designs and styles but in brief, it is simply ground coffee with hot water running through it under gravity. This is my favourite brewing method and as before, you use three variables to control the result for proper coffee.

Filter Coffee
Dose = 60g Time = 4-5 minutes Yield = 1litre

Top Tip:
The ground coffee should feel like gritty like sand. This recipe is super simple, and the quantities can be increased or decreased depending on the volume of brew you want to make. For example, if you only want to make 500ml of filter coffee, only use 30g of ground coffee.

Dose
This means how much coffee you put in your filter method. This method works really well with lighter roasts but this is a preference not a rule.

Time
This is as simple as starting a stopwatch when you press your brew and stopping it when the brew has finished. Be warned, this is the hard part!

Yield
This means how much filter coffee comes out. Use weighing scales to get an accurate result and remember that for coffee, millilitres weigh the same as grams so if your scales say 500g this means you have 500ml of filter coffee.

Brewing Goals
The aim is to have all three variables (dose, time and yield) in line with the recipe above. The dose and yield can be controlled by simply weighing the coffee accurately, but the key to great filter coffee is to make sure you add the water in stages, not all at once.

HOW TO BREW PROPER COFFEE -CAFETIERE

This is probably the most common coffee maker we see in Yorkshire; everyone has one in the back of the cupboard!

Cafetiere
Dose = 60g Time = 5-7 minutes Yield = 1 1litre

Top Tip:
The ground coffee should feel like gritty sea salt, very coarse.

Dose
This means how much coffee you put in the cafetiere before brewing.

Time
This is as simple as starting a stopwatch when you press your brew and stopping it when the brew has finished. Time is your friend here in my opinion, as this method is better the longer you leave it, so don't rush it.

Yield
This means how much coffee comes out. Use weighing scales to get an accurate result and remember that for coffee, millilitres weigh the same as grams so if your scales say 700g this means you have 700ml of brewed coffee.

Brewing Goals
The aim is to have all three variables (dose, time and yield) in line with the recipe above. The dose and yield can be controlled by simply weighing the coffee accurately, but the key is letting this brew take its time, as the longer you leave it, the more depth of flavour you will get.

RELISH THE FLAVOUR

Hendersons (Sheffield) Ltd has been making Henderson's Relish since 1885. It remains an independent, family-owned business, and is still blending and bottling Sheffield's famous sauce to its secret recipe.

The Freeman family has owned Henderson's for three generations. But really, Henderson's Relish belongs to Sheffield. It's all of ours. Whether you've just arrived, have been here for years, or have never left, there's something about this city's spicy sauce that is different, just right.

Splash it on pies, stews and cheese on toast: Henderson's Relish is surely the city's favourite table sauce. Much more than a condiment, it's an essential ingredient too. From home cooks to Michelin-starred chefs, Henderson's is for everyone. It's vegetarian, vegan and gluten-free. As the local comedian Tom Wrigglesworth says, 'outsiders think Henderson's Relish is Sheffield's answer to Worcester Sauce. In Sheffield, we think it's the answer to everything'.

The story of Henderson's Relish began in 1885, at the general store of chemist Henry Henderson. Henry would blend ingredients to create mixtures to sell from his premises on Broad Lane, and Relish was first sold from large wooden barrels in the back of the shop. As word spread, customers would bring their own glass bottles to be filled for just a penny apiece.

Over the last 137 years, much has changed, of course. Today, Henderson's Relish is mixed in 1000 litre drums, and its own embossed bottles speed down the production line to be filled and capped by machine. But much remains the same, too. Henderson's Relish is made in Sheffield. Its bright orange label still stands out from the crowd, and its family owners are still mixing and guarding the secret recipe.

The city of Sheffield is changing and growing. Our food reflects not only our history, but the influence of diverse cultures and the demands of modern lifestyles. Yet Henderson's Relish remains and thrives, because when you find Henderson's Relish, you discover something of Sheffield. A surprise, perhaps? Unique, certainly! But always strong, and full of flavour. Once you try it, you can't help but love it.

HENDERSONS (SHEFFIELD) LTD
MAKERS OF
HENDERSON'S
RELISH
Made in Sheffield for over 100 years

HENDERSON'S RELISH
ESTD 1885
HENDO'S
SOYA & POTATO
SPICY SNACK
STRONG & NORTHERN
VEGAN
GLUTEN FREE

HENDERSON'S
STRONG & NORTHERN
RELISH

MADE IN SHEFFIELD
ESTD 1885
NG & NORTHERN
THE SPICY TABLE SAUCE
MADE TO A SECRET
FAMILY RECIPE

HENDERSON'S
STRONG & NORTHERN

HENDERSON'S
ESTD 1885
STRONG & NORTHERN
RELISH

LUCA'S BURNT AUBERGINE CHILLI

Preparation time: 10 minutes | Cooking time: 1 hour 50 minutes | Serves 4

The smoky flavour of this chilli comes from charring the aubergine before adding it to a base of beans and lentils, creating a warming dish that makes a lovely change from your usual veggie or bean chilli.

1 aubergine
1 tbsp olive oil
1 red onion, diced
2 carrots, diced
2 cloves of garlic, finely chopped
50g red lentils
75g green lentils
400g canned kidney beans
400g chopped tinned tomatoes
25g vegan dark chocolate
3 tbsp Henderson's Relish
2 tbsp tomato purée
2 tsp smoked paprika
2 tsp ground cumin
1 tsp ground coriander
1 tsp ground cinnamon
½ tsp chilli powder
750ml vegetable stock
1 lime, juiced

Use a gas hob, barbecue or heat the grill to char the skin of the aubergine, turning occasionally, until completely blackened. Remove from the heat and set aside to cool, then peel off the charred skin and remove the stem until you are left with just the flesh. Roughly chop and set aside.

In a pan, heat the oil and then add the onion, carrots and garlic. Fry over a low-medium heat for 10 minutes, stirring constantly, until the vegetables have softened.

Add the aubergine, lentils, kidney beans, tinned tomatoes, vegan dark chocolate, Henderson's Relish, tomato purée, smoked paprika, cumin, coriander, cinnamon, and chilli powder. Stir well, then pour in the stock. Bring to the boil, then turn down to a low heat. Cover and cook for 1 hour, checking and stirring every 15 minutes to prevent it from sticking to the pan.

After an hour, remove the lid and let the mixture simmer over a fairly low heat, stirring occasionally, for about 20 minutes until the sauce thickens. Stir in the lime juice and season to taste. Serve hot over rice or couscous with guacamole, vegan sour cream and grated vegan cheese. Splash on some more Henderson's Relish to taste and enjoy!

LUKE FRENCH'S MEAT & POTATO PIE

Preparation time: 1-2 hours | Cooking time: 4 hours | Serves 8

Why make an ordinary meat and potato pie when you can elevate it to the next level with amazing ingredients and a bit of extra time and effort? This recipe was created by the chef director of JÖRO and uses Sheffield's very own wagyu beef along with Henderson's Relish for a weekend treat that's sure to impress.

For the pie filling

900g Wortley wagyu braising steak, diced
8g table salt
75g each plain flour & beef dripping
250g diced white onion
175g peeled and diced carrot
110g diced shiitake mushroom (stalks removed)
20g peeled and diced garlic
330g IPA
450g each fresh beef stock and dark chicken stock
200g tinned chopped tomatoes
50g double concentrated tomato purée
5g dried ma-kombu seaweed
2g fresh thyme leaves
900g peeled and diced waxy potatoes
150g Henderson's Relish
20g caster sugar
25g IPA vinegar
25g flat leaf parsley, chopped

For the pastry

230g wild farmed all-purpose flour
490g unsalted butter, diced and frozen
35g beef dripping
9g table salt & 175g cold water
1 egg yolk + 50ml milk, whisked

For the pie filling

Heat a cast iron casserole dish over a medium heat while you toss the beef in the salt and flour. Melt the dripping in the casserole dish and brown the beef all over in 3 batches. Remove the beef from the pan and set aside. Cook the onion, carrot, mushroom and garlic in the casserole dish until golden and caramelised, stirring regularly. Add the beef back to the pan and stir it in. Add the IPA and bring to the boil, then add the stocks, tomatoes and purée. Rinse the seaweed under cold water for 30 seconds, then stir in along with the thyme.

Transfer the casserole dish to a preheated oven at 160°c fan for 1 hour 30 minutes. After this time, give the mix a good stir and increase the oven temperature to 180°c fan. Place a lid on the casserole dish and cook for a further 40 minutes. Meanwhile, cook the potatoes until tender when pierced with a knife and leave to cool. Remove the casserole dish from the oven and stir in the Henderson's Relish, IPA vinegar, sugar, potatoes and parsley. Allow the filling to cool.

For the pastry

Combine half the flour with the butter and dripping using the paddle attachment in a stand mixer or food processor (or rub together by hand) until breadcrumb-like. Stir in the remaining flour and salt, then add the cold water and mix to form a dough.

Remove from the bowl and knead gently for 2 minutes, then roll the dough into a ball and press it into a flat disc about 1 inch thick. Wrap this in cling film and refrigerate for at least 1 hour.

Preheat the oven to 180°c fan and grease two 25cm pie tins with beef dripping, butter, or cooking spray. Divide the pastry into quarters and roll them into 3mm thick rounds on a cold surface lightly dusted with flour. Line the greased tins with a round of pastry, pressing it gently into the edges. Fill them with the cooled filling. Now place the tops on and crimp the pastry together at the edges using your fingers. Brush the tops with a little egg wash and then cut a little steam hole in the middle of each pie. Bake in the preheated oven for 30-45 minutes or until golden brown and piping hot in the centre. Allow the pies to cool slightly before serving with your favourite sides and some more Henderson's Relish to splash on at the table.

HENDERSONS
RELISH

NORTH TOWN'S GLUTEN-FREE PORK, BEEF & SAUSAGE RAGU

Preparation time: 10 minutes | Cooking time: 2 hours | Serves 2

This is our classic slow cooked North Town ragu made using the finest Sicilian fennel sausages (which are naturally gluten-free) and heightened with the one and only Hendo's!

25ml olive oil
1 carrot
1 small white onion
1 stick of celery
4 cloves of garlic
30g diced smoked pancetta
100g Sicilian fennel sausage (taken out of the casing)
150g pork mince
150g beef mince
50ml Henderson's Relish plus more for dousing later!
400g tinned San Marzano tomatoes, blended to a passata consistency
5g salt and pepper, or to taste
180g Gragnano gluten-free pasta (available from North Town)

Start by preparing your soffritto (onion, celery, carrot). First, peel, top and tail the carrot and dice small. Next, peel and finely dice the onion. Wash the celery stick and finely dice that too. Peel and finely chop the garlic cloves. Meanwhile, put a medium-size stock pan on a medium to high heat. Once the pan is hot, add the olive oil and garlic, cooking it for 30 seconds before adding in the diced soffritto you prepared earlier. Keep stirring until it has sweated down and the onion and celery have become translucent.

Next, add the pancetta and the fennel sausage meat. Stir to break up the sausage meat as well as you can and keep cooking until both start to brown. Once they are brown, add the pork and beef mince and mix thoroughly in the pan. Liquid will come out of the mince so continue to cook until it simmers away, stirring regularly to break up the mince. Once the liquid has evaporated, continue to cook the mince until it starts to brown.

Now add the Henderson's Relish to deglaze the pan and get all those sticky caramelised flavours up from the base. Take a moment to take in those gorgeous smells from the Hendo's and meats working together! Next, add the blended San Marzano tomatoes and stir everything together. Turn the heat down to low, loosely cover the pan with a lid and leave the ragu to cook for 1-1.5 hours. Check and stir it periodically, making sure the heat is not too aggressive and it's not catching on the bottom of the pan.

When the ragu is nearly ready, put a pan of salted water on to boil for the pasta. Once the water is boiling, tip in the gluten-free pasta (we use a Naples Gragnano Caserecce at the moment) and stir, then turn the heat down to medium and cook for 9 minutes. Drain the pasta, reserving an espresso cup (30ml) of the cooking water.

Mix the pasta with the ragu, a splash of the pasta water and a good pinch of black pepper. Split between two bowls, grate over some parmesan cheese and of course liberally douse in the Henderson's Relish! Buon Appetito.

HENDERSON'S
ESTD 1885
STRONG & NORTHERN
RELISH

FROM EAST TO WEST

Hungry Buddha's owner, founder and chef has been on a long trek to establish his successful Nepalese street food café in the Moor Market...

Dev was born and raised in Kathmandu, Nepal. He worked as a trekking guide, leading treks in the Nepalese and Indian Himalayas where he met some lovely, adventurous, happy people brought together through a common interest in the challenge. He has walked two of the most sought-after trekking routes in the world: Everest and Annapurna.

It was while working as a trekking guide in Nepal that Dev met Jan. She was in the group he was guiding at Gokyo, circa 5,300 metres up with an awe-inspiring 360-degree vista. This chance encounter led to Dev arriving in Sheffield to be with Jan. The one thing he missed more than anything was good traditional Nepalese home-cooked food, especially his mum's cooking. He started experimenting, trying to recreate the flavours and aromas from his childhood with a little help from the folks back home, who gave him lots of tips and recipes.

Dev decided to train for a career as a chef, and after finishing college he joined the Bombay Bicycle Club in London, and worked in several Nepalese, Indian and British eateries in Sheffield, London, Birmingham and Litchfield. Then in 2016 he took the plunge and started Hungry Buddha, the authentic Nepalese street food café in Sheffield's Moor Market.

Hungry Buddha brings home-cooked, flavoursome, subtly spiced, fresh Nepalese food to Sheffield. The ethos is about simple spicing and the use of seasonal ingredients, and all the food is cooked fresh on the day. The café, where you can eat in or take out, aims to showcase Nepalese food served on a thali plate, buffet style. It also offers the most popular street food in Nepal: momo. These are steamed bitesize dumplings with a chicken or vegetable filling, served with chilli and tomato or sesame dipping chutney. Hungry Buddha offers two different vegan or vegetarian curry options and one meat option every day depending on what produce is available on the day and season.

HAND MADE
IN NEPAL

The
Moor
Market
Sheffield
Drop-in vaccination clinic here

HUNGRY
BUDDHA
www.hungrybuddha.co.uk

HUNGRY
BUDDHA
TRADITIONAL
NEPALESE FOOD
LIKE YOU'VE NEVER
TASTED BEFORE

DAL BHAT TARKARI

Preparation time: 2 hours | Cooking time: 30-40 minutes | Serves 4

The main staple diet of most Nepali people is dal, bhat and tarkari which translates as lentils, rice and curried vegetables. This combination is also known as the 'holy trinity' with the addition of meat during special occasions. Here, the tarkari is a pea and potato curry.

For the dal

500g chana dal
6 tbsp vegetable oil
1 tsp cumin seeds
1 sun-dried chilli
1 tbsp ginger-garlic paste (4cm fresh ginger + 2 large cloves of garlic, very finely chopped)
1 tbsp ground turmeric
Salt and pepper, to taste

For the tarkari

3 medium potatoes, peeled and chopped into bite-size pieces
3 tbsp vegetable oil
½ tbsp cumin seeds
½ sun-dried chilli
1 tbsp ginger-garlic paste (4cm fresh ginger + 2 large cloves of garlic, very finely chopped)
1 tsp ground turmeric
1 large brown onion, finely chopped
2 medium tomatoes, finely chopped
1 tsp each ground coriander, ground cumin, chilli powder & garam masala
75g green peas, boiled or frozen
1 tbsp lemon or lime juice

For the dal

Rinse the chana dal a few times until the water runs clear, then drain the lentils and place in a pan with double the volume of water. Bring to the boil, then cover and reduce the heat to a simmer. Stir occasionally, skimming off the froth that forms on the surface. Cook for 30-40 minutes until the lentils are soft and tender, adding more water if needed. Once cooked, use a hand blender to blitz the dal into a soupy consistency.

Heat the oil in a frying pan until hot. Add the cumin seeds, chilli, ginger-garlic paste and turmeric. Be careful as it will sizzle. When the ingredients start to change colour, add them to the dal. Add water to achieve your desired consistency. Bring it back to the boil, then add salt and pepper to taste.

You can cook this dal in advance and freeze in individual containers. You can also freeze the ginger-garlic paste in ice cube trays covered with sealed plastic bags.

For the tarkari

Peel the potatoes and chop them into bite-size pieces, then place in a pan and cover with double the volume of water. Bring to a rolling boil, then cover the pan and lower the heat. Simmer for 15-20 minutes until tender.

Heat the oil in a medium, heavy-bottomed, lidded pan. When the oil is hot, add the cumin seeds, sun-dried chilli and ginger-garlic paste. When they change colour, add the turmeric. This might sizzle and end up burnt if left for too long, so act fast. Add the onion and tomato, stir well, cover with a lid and cook for 5 minutes. Add the remaining spices, then stir and cover to cook for another 5 minutes. Add a little hot water if the mixture is looking dry. Stir in the potatoes and peas and cook for a final 5 minutes, then add the lemon or lime juice and season with salt and pepper to taste.

Serve with boiled rice and fresh chopped coriander.

MOMO

Preparation time: 1 hour | Cooking time: 13 minutes | Makes about 25

These steamed bite-size dumplings are the most popular street food in Nepal. You can make vegetarian momos by substituting the chicken with any veg filling. Popular fillings in Nepal include mushroom, tofu, paneer, cabbage, spinach, carrot, cauliflower or a mixture.

For the dough

200g Maida flour (finely milled refined and bleached wheat flour, available at southeast Asian stores, or you can substitute this process with ready-made dumpling wrappers)
80ml lukewarm water
Pinch of salt

For the filling

250g lean minced chicken
3 tbsp finely chopped spring onion
2 tbsp chopped fresh coriander
1 tbsp lemon or lime juice
1 fresh green chilli, finely chopped
1 tsp salt
½ tbsp ground cumin
½ tbsp ground coriander
½ tbsp garam masala
Salt and pepper to taste

For the tempering

5 tbsp cooking oil
5 pieces fenugreek seeds
1 sun-dried chilli
1 tbsp ginger-garlic paste

For the dough

Add the Maida flour and salt to a bowl, make a well in centre and add the water. Mix to form a dough. Add more water if it looks dry. Knead for about 5 minutes until smooth, soft and elastic. Cover and rest for 15-20 minutes.

To make the wrapper, shape the dough into 25 individual balls that are 2.5cm in diameter. Flour your work surface, flatten the balls and roll each one into an 8cm diameter circle. Aim to start from the middle and roll away from you. Turn and roll the other side until you get a round wrapper. Aim to reach a similar consistency of the dough throughout. Cover with a damp tea towel if it starts to feel dry.

For the filling

In a metal bowl, bring all the ingredients together. For tempering, heat the cooking oil until nearly smoking. Add the fenugreek seeds, then as soon as they start to change colour, add the chilli and ginger-garlic paste. It should be sizzling. Pour this mixture over the filling and mix well, adding salt and pepper to taste.

To make the momo

Take a wrapper and put a teaspoon of filling in the centre. One of the most popular shapes of dumplings in Nepal are full moon. Your thumb, index and middle finger play a big part here. Keeping the filling in the centre, pinch and make a pleat using your thumb and index finger. As the thumb and index is holding the pinch, use the middle finger to draw in the wrapper edge towards the index finger. As your middle finger draws in, remove your index finger, so that the next pleat joins together with a pinch. Replace your middle finger with your index, so that the middle finger repeats the process. As the pleats come together, a full moon shape will form. Make sure that the wrapper is totally enclosing the filling.

Steam the momo for 13 minutes, then serve with chilli sauce or tomato and sesame chutney.

If you are not sure about any of the processes in this recipe, you can find many YouTube videos on the various topics covered here. Or, come down to Hungry Buddha at the Moor Market and we will point you in the right direction.

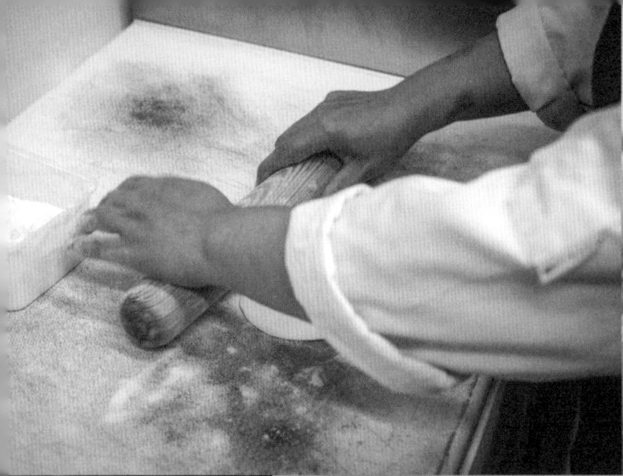

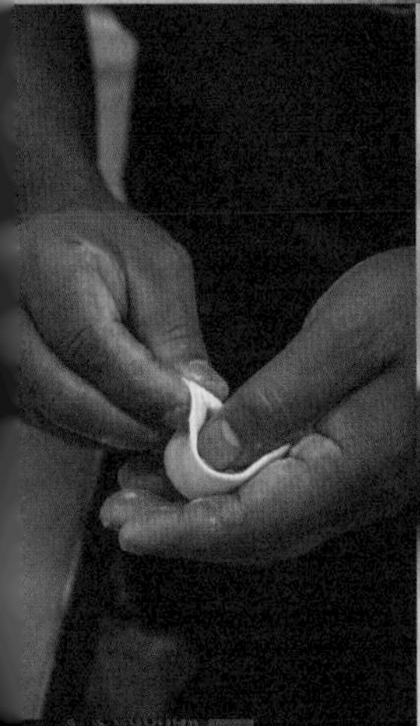
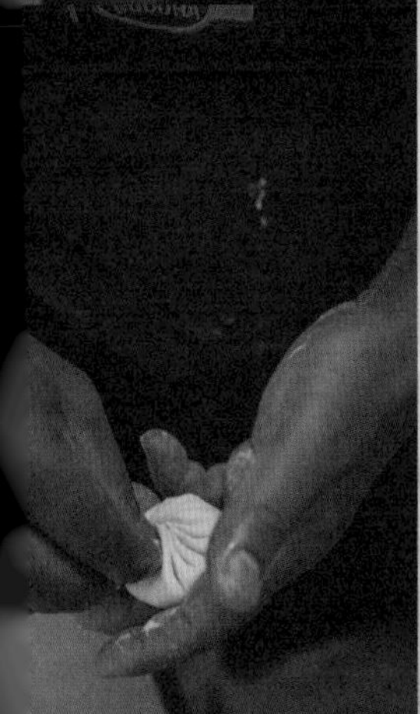
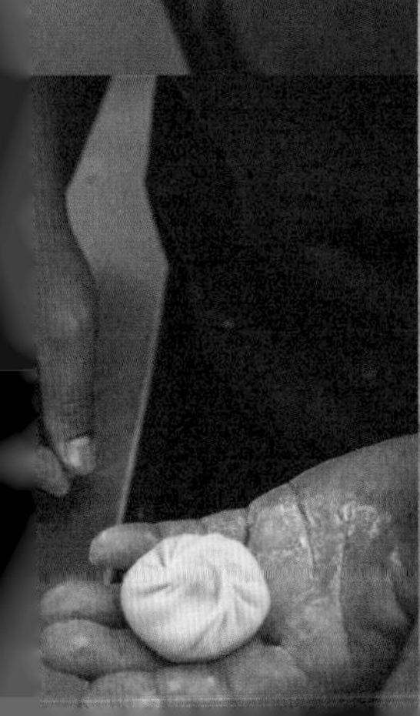

A HIVE OF INDUSTRY

Tucked away in the Cultural Industries Quarter, The Industry Tap is a cosy beer lovers dream.

It's all about choice at the Industry Tap. Whether you're a matchday reveller or a beer ticking connoisseur (or both!), with a whopping 21 lines there's a beer for everyone at this truly independent, Sidney Street boozer.

Recently celebrating its third birthday, the Tap has become a firm Sheffield favourite for everything from a quiet evening pint to grabbing a couple of cans from its stacked fridges, or even the perfect venue to hire out for that special occasion.

Showcasing brews from some of the world's finest craft beer brands, as well as local and UK-wide gems, the dog-friendly bar has you well-covered whether you're looking for a big Belgian beauty, something a little lighter on the palate, or even a gluten or alcohol-free option.

A glance up at the two screens, which hang above the bar, provides details of stouts or imperial stouts, IPAs or double IPAs, sours and even premium ciders, on occasion.

Within their broad range of styles, local breweries are well represented with Sheffield favourites like Abbeydale, Triple Point, Little Mesters and SMOD all getting a look in alongside industry darlings like DEYA, and even more unusual fare from further afield.

They also boast a wide selection of spirits and cocktails if that's more your thing, and just to make sure they have all the bases covered, they always offer a top-quality, premium lager on draught.

"We try to keep things a little bit different," says Industry Tap owner Darren Filsell, "I'm very big on working with breweries direct and trying to get stuff that's not been in Sheffield before and I've got a fantastic team who are all very into their beers."

Darren's knowledgeable team, which includes Dale, Lewis and Jack, all have plenty of experience in the hospitality industry and local breweries, making sure you're in for a welcoming experience, where you don't have to be an expert to enjoy what's on offer.

All this is before we get to the comfy interiors and glorious terrace suntrap. Darren and his team have worked tirelessly over the past few years to make sure the unusually shaped, triangular space feels homely and comfortable, and more importantly the perfect place to enjoy a scoop or two.

We all have plenty of choices to make in life but seeking out the Industry Tap bar is definitely one you won't regret.

INDUSTRY
tap

INDUSTRY
tap

BEER PAIRINGS

While beer pairing can be a science, we have suggested some beers and styles that we feel will complement some of the dishes from this book. There are lots of breweries doing all the styles below, so we have showcased some that we feel will be accessible to everyone.

Aesthete – Nutella Gateau

Pairing Style: Fruit Beer

Suggested Beer: Cherry Chouffe

Notes: The aroma of Cherry Chouffe gives pride of place to cherries. It also reveals notes of strawberry, almond, spices and sweet Port. Round-bodied, soft and delicate, it has a satisfying finish, with a very slight bitterness.

Akentannos – Cervo alle Erbe Aromatiche

Pairing Style: Stout

Suggested Beer: Nerd Brewing

Notes: Collab with Emperors Brewery. Imperial stout brewed with maple syrup and aged on toasted coconut shreds.

Akentannos – Fregola ai Frutti di Mare

Pairing Style: Witbier

Suggested Beer: Round Corner Brewing Zomba

Notes: Delicate yet complex, Zomba pours hazy white with a thick white pillowy head. Incredibly fragrant, this stunning Belgian witbier yeast strain delivers aromas of juicy fruit, Skittles, Turkish delight and gentle phenolics. Orange zest and lime character from coriander seed lift the refreshing citrus character and are under-pinned by a subtle lavender flower aroma.

Bench – Grilled Pork Collar Steak with Rebel XO

Pairing Style: Belgian Blond

Suggested Beer: La Chouffe

Notes: Slight hoppy taste, combining notes of fresh coriander and fruity tones.

Bullion – Chocolate Brownie

Pairing Style: Stout or Fruit Lambic

Suggested Beer: Kriek Boon

Notes: The cherries and young lambic create a red beer that is both natural and fresh, with an absolutely unforgettable sweet and sour taste. This is kriek as it should be, with nothing but real cherries and lambic.

Doughboy – Chocolate Chip Cookies

Pairing Style: Belgian Dubbel

Suggested Beer: Westmalle Dubbel

Notes: Dark, reddish-brown Trappist beer with a secondary fermentation in the bottle. The creamy head has the fragrance of special malt. The flavour is rich and complex, herby and fruity with a fresh-bitter finish.

Dysh – Pistachio and Cherry Bakewell Tart

Pairing Style: Fruit Sour

Suggested Beer: Elmeleven Fruited Sour Ale or Lost Industry Annum Sour

Notes: Fruited sour ale with passionfruit, pear, blackcurrant and vanilla.

Henderson's Relish – Meat & Potato Pie by Luke French

Pairing Style: Trappist Beer

Suggested Beer: Trappistes Rochefort 10 or Tynt Meadow

Notes: Rochefort 10 gives a dominant impressions of latte coffee with powerful chocolate aromas in the nose. The alcohol esters are enveloped with hints of autumn wood, citrus zest and freshly baked biscuits. The initial taste is sweetly sinful. Beer and chocolate in a single glass: a liquid milky draught with a backbone of bitter malt. The alcohol warms the throat and you'll pick up traces of cloves, citrus, orange and mocha.

Duvel
666

Duvel
666
Duvel
TRIPEL HOP CITRA
LA CHOUFFE

BOON
KRIEK
BOON
PEACH
LA CHOUFFE

Tripel
Trappistes
Rochefort
10
CERVEZA
TRAPPIST
DUBBEL
LA CHOUFFE

666
Duvel
666

BEER PAIRINGS

Konjo – Korean Fried Chicken

Pairing Style: Lager or Pils

Suggested Beer: Abbeydale Heresy or Kernal Pils

Notes: Abbeydale Heresy is a clean and crisp sessionable lager in the continental style, with a fresh and floral aroma. Noble hops and low bitterness provide an easy drinking beer with a clear and bright presence in the glass. (GF)

Konjo – Crispy Shredded Chilli Beef

Pairing Style: Stout

Suggested Beer: Round Corner Brewing Reverend Hooker

Notes: A smooth, creamy, dry Irish stout. Pouring black with a tight white head, toasted malt and dried fruit aromas merge with earthy hop notes and evolve into a sublimely smooth, silky palate. Luscious roast malt characters of coffee and toast make way for a long and noble bitterness and delectably dry finish.

Konjo – Chicken Katsu Bao

Pairing Style: Golden Ale

Suggested Beer: Round Corner Brewing Steeplechase or Thornbridge Zero Five

Notes: Steeplechase pours a sumptuous orange hue provided by a base of the finest English barley malts. Builds a level of sweet malt complexity that is well balanced with New Zealand and US hops. Juicy hop aromas of oranges, tropical fruit and citrus orchards lead to a very pleasing bitterness and cleansing finish.

La Mama - Sopaipillas and Pebre

Pairing Style: Flanders Red Ale

Suggested Beer: Duchesse De Bourgogne

Notes: Traditional Flemish red ale. This refreshing ale is matured in oak casks, smooth with a rich texture and interplay of passionfruit and chocolate, and a long, dry and acidic finish.

Luca – Beef Shin Ragu

Pairing Style: Stout

Suggested Beer: SMOD Babayaga

Notes: Slight smoky Sylvan stout. Rich, dark, with a hint of smoke.

China Red – Poached Beef in Hot Chilli Oil

Pairing Style: Saison

Suggested Beer: Saison Dupont

Notes: A world classic beer, straw coloured with a dense creamy head. The nose is alive, like fresh raised bread, esters with citrus and spice notes. Full-bodied and malty, it sparkles on the palate and finishes with a zesty hop and citrus attack.

China Red – Gong-Po Chicken

Pairing Style: Weissbier

Suggested Beer: Weihenstephaner Heffe Weissbier

Notes: This golden-yellow wheat beer, with its fine-pored white foam, smells of cloves and impresses with its refreshing banana flavour. It is full bodied with a smooth yeast taste.

Omega at Abbeydale – Assiette of Fish with Sultana Rice and Lentil Dahl

Pairing Style: IPA

Suggested Beer: Abbeydale Voyager IPA

Notes: A big American style IPA, oozing juicy citrus and tropical fruit flavours with a vibrant finish. West Coast bitterness meets East Coast fruitiness with a trio of mega hops Citra, Centennial and Mosaic. (GF)

Omega at Abbeydale – Braised Pig's Cheeks with Kidney, Apple Purée and Mash

Pairing Style: Blond

Suggested Beer: Duval 666

Notes: Let yourself be swept away by the dance of the hop devils, inspired by the fruity aroma of the hops and zesty orange. Malted barley and malted wheat with six refined hop varieties.

ROUND CORNER BREWING
STEEPLECHASE
PALE ALE
ALC 4.4% VOL
ROUND CORNER BREWING
REVEREND
HOOKER
IRISH STOUT
ALC 5.5% VOL

HERESY
LAGER
HEATHEN
AMERICAN PALE ALE
VOYAGER
ROUND CORNER
BULLROARER
STEEPLECHASE
PALE ALE
ALC 4.4%

JEDI MINDTRICK
Three Hills
NERDBREWING
YODA
CONDITION
330ML ALC 12.3%VOL
ROUND CORNER BREWING
REVEREND
HOOKER
IRISH STOUT
ALC 5.5% VOL

Weihenstephaner
HEFE
WEISSBIER
THE KERNEL
PILS
ZERO
FIVE
VEDETT

VEDETT

PAR-TEA TIME

Jameson's Tea Rooms & Kitchens is a popular Sheffield institution, adding a touch of class to your afternoon tea.

There couldn't be a better home for Jameson's Tea Rooms & Kitchens than the middle of Sheffield's antiques quarter. The Jameson family name has been known in the city's antique business since 1883, so it perhaps came as no surprise when, back in 2012, a traditional tearoom bearing its name opened its doors on Abbeydale Road.

The resurgence of the road in recent years, following a spate of new bar openings, has only added to the destination's popularity and customers come from far and wide to enjoy the finest afternoon tea and exceptional customer service. As you walk through the doors, chandeliers decorate the ceiling, and customers are greeted with a friendliness and warmth that is often overlooked in the rush of modern life. While the venue offers a nod to a bygone era, the tearoom is far from a stuffy time capsule, giving an elegant, contemporary twist to a classic British staple, as well as being the perfect venue for birthdays, baby showers, hen parties and anything else you feel like celebrating with an exquisite cuppa.

Afternoon tea is, as you would expect, the heart of the business with seven different afternoon teas available ranging from 'traditional' right up to 'regal' with a bottle of Pol Roger Champagne, as well as a 'little ladies and gents' version. Afternoon tea is not all that's on the (white linen-adorned) table either; they also pride themselves on the quality of their home baked cakes, scones, breakfast, brunches, and delightful lunches, which keep people coming back for more.

"We've been told we do the best Ploughman's Lunch people have ever had! People come here for an experience," says owner Suzy Pitchley. They might come for a birthday or a celebration to have our afternoon tea, and then they keep on coming back. People tell us we offer the best afternoon tea around and it's down to the customer service. We make it special."

It's not just about food and tea either, as the newest version of its in-house shop, Jameson's Gifts & Antiques, is more accessible than ever before and offers something a little bit different, with a focus on high quality local producers and makers. Having moved back into the same building as Jameson's Tea Rooms & Kitchens, on the first floor, the shop is now more closely linked with its sister business and shares the relaxed atmosphere. Customers can have a browse before enjoying afternoon tea, or pop upstairs after a coffee to find the perfect present, wrapping paper and card in one place.

HAPPINESS IS
LOVE
LOVE

Jameson's
Jameson's
TEAROOM & KITCHENS

Jameson's
Cocktails

wilberry

BAKED AVOCADO EGGS WITH WARM TOMATO, CHORIZO & RED PEPPER RELISH

Preparation time: 15 minutes | Cooking time: 20 minutes | Serves 2

A contemporary twist on our very popular 'avocado and eggs' dish for the perfect, healthy breakfast, brunch or lunchtime feast.

1 tsp olive oil
1 large red pepper, diced
8 slices of chorizo, 4 chopped and 4 left whole (optional)
1 x 400g tin of finely chopped tomatoes
Pinch of smoked paprika
Pinch of dried oregano
Pinch of chilli flakes
½ tsp sugar
Salt and pepper
2 avocados
4 medium eggs
2 slices of sourdough
100g feta cheese
1 fresh red chilli, chopped
Spring onion, green parts finely chopped

Preheat the oven to 180°c. Heat the olive oil in a pan and sauté the red pepper. Once softened, add the chopped chorizo (if using) and cook for 3-4 minutes.

Add the chopped tomatoes, paprika, oregano, chilli flakes, sugar, salt and pepper to the pan. Stir well and cook for a further 15 minutes.

Meanwhile, halve the avocados and remove the stones. Place the avocado into a baking dish and carefully break 1 egg into each half. You may need to scoop a small amount of flesh out of the avocado first to accommodate the egg, depending on the size of the stone you removed.

Place an ovenproof dish filled with boiling water in the bottom of the oven, then place the avocados on the shelf above to bake for 12-15 minutes, so the egg yolk is still runny but the white is set.

Grill the remaining chorizo slices (if using) until slightly crispy and toast the sourdough bread.

Place 2 avocado halves on each plate and top with the crumbled feta, fresh chilli (to taste) and chopped spring onion greens. In a separate small bowl, add some of the warm tomato relish and top with the crispy chorizo slices. Serve the baked avocado eggs and relish with the buttered sourdough.

FEELIN' HOT, HOT, HOT

Alex Khoo's hot sauce journey began with a love of music, food and experimental cooking...

A keen home cook, Alex had always leaned into creating sauces because there's so much room for experimenting with different flavours. He was also getting into the geeky side of growing his own chillies, discovering varieties that you couldn't buy fresh in the UK and learning about the enormous (and mostly untapped) flavour potential of this key ingredient. As part of the York music scene in his early twenties, Alex often hosted barbecues for the other DJs, who would try these homemade sauces. More and more, friends started suggesting that Alex should sell them and eventually, he did.

Khoo's Hot Sauce was established in 2012 and has since become Alex's full-time job, alongside raising his young daughter with his wife Amy. The whole venture is run from home, with all the sauces cooked by Alex himself in their home kitchen and packed in their repurposed attic room. Inspired by Sheffield's independent spirit and the Little Mester mentality of keeping things in-house, Alex also credits Amy for the business' existence: from setting up at markets, labelling bottles at all hours and working in their chilli-growing polytunnel, she has been integral to Khoo's Hot Sauce from the beginning. Alex's dad, a mechanic, also plays a large part by creating custom smokers with him, making this small producer a true family affair.

With seven hot sauces in the core range and a Pitmaster's Finest collection of barbecue condiments, business is thriving and the recipes are always evolving. Alex tries to source all his chillies from UK farms, having outgrown his own polytunnel due to demand, which is now a hub for product development. This approach reduces his environmental impact, as does using completely compostable packaging for the UK-wide mail order service and glass bottles for all Khoo's Hot Sauce products. They are stocked in lots of local shops including Coles Corner, The Green Shop and Beeches of Walkley, and business boomed after a feature on the Hairy Bikers' Go North for Christmas TV programme in 2021.

Khoo's distinctive branding is something that Alex is really proud of, again going back to his roots in music: both illustrators – Yorkshire-born Hazard for the core range and Dutch artist Tom Hamel for Pitmasters – met Alex through shared tastes in hip hop and hardcore respectively. "It's always been really important that my product looks as good as it tastes," explains Alex, demonstrating his passion for every element of the business. With new chillies to be grown and tasted, sauces to be developed and Sheffield behind him all the way, the future of Khoo's looks like pretty hot stuff!

CHILLI AND LIME MEXICAN PORK SHOULDER

Preparation time: 20 minutes | Cooking time: 7 hours | Serves 4

This is not your average pulled pork. Fiery, succulent, satisfyingly crispy around the edges, and a perfect match for tacos. For tender pork that melts in your mouth, either slowly roast in the oven or, to add extra depth to the flavour, cook over wood in your smoker or kettle barbecue.

2kg boneless pork shoulder

For the bind

Smoker Method

50ml Khoo's Northern Beacon hot sauce

1 lime, zested

Oven Method

30ml Khoo's Northern Beacon hot sauce

20ml Khoo's Heavy Smoker chipotle sauce

1 lime, zested

For the rub

2 guajillo chillies, coarsely ground or 2 tbsp chilli flakes

4 tsp coarse black pepper

4 tsp garlic powder

3 tsp sea salt

2 tsp each smoked paprika & cumin

For the spritz

200ml each apple & lime juice

For the baste

Smoker Method

30ml Khoo's Northern Beacon hot sauce

1 lime, juiced

Oven Method

20ml Khoo's Northern Beacon hot sauce

20ml Khoo's Heavy Smoker chipotle sauce

1 lime, juiced

Remove the skin from the pork shoulder and save it for later. Combine the 'bind' ingredients for your chosen cooking method and rub the bind into the joint, making sure to cover it completely.

Combine the 'rub' ingredients and dust onto all sides of the pork joint, making sure to cover it completely.

If you are using a smoker or barbecue, build your fire using apple or cherry wood. Preheat your chamber to 120°c. Otherwise, preheat the oven to 120°c.

Combine the spritz ingredients in a spray bottle. Cook the pork in the preheated smoker or oven for 3 hours at 120°c, spritzing with the mixture in the spray bottle every 45 minutes.

Remove the pork from the smoker or oven, combine the 'baste' ingredients for your chosen cooking method and brush all over the joint. Retire the smoker at this point, as the meat has taken all the smoke it needs. Wrap in two layers of tin foil and cook in the oven for a further 3 hours at 120°c.

Salt the reserved pork skin and add to the oven on a separate tray. After 3 hours, unwrap the pork, and place on a roasting tray. Spritz and return to the oven unwrapped at 120°c for 1 hour. Keep an eye on it and remove from oven when the outside of the meat has taken on a dark brown crust.

Pull the joint into chunks and serve in tortillas with mango salsa and pickled red onions. Finely chop the crispy pork skin and add to the tortillas for extra crunch.

KHOO'S
HOT SAUCE
CAUTION HOT
THE NORTHERN BEACON
HOT SAUCE
CHILLI RATING
HANDMADE IN SHEFFIELD

CARAMELISED MANGO CHILLI SALSA

Preparation time: 20 minutes | Cooking time: 10 minutes | Serves 4

Blackened mango and lime combine with our apricot and chilli Super Sauce to deliver a sweet, tangy and punchy salsa ready to level up any Mexican meal.

1 medium red onion
Handful of fresh coriander leaves
2 limes, zested and juiced
40ml Khoo's Super Sauce
1 clove of garlic, minced
1 tsp cracked black pepper
3 large red sweet peppers
2 underripe mangos
2 tbsp olive oil
Sea salt, to taste

Finely chop the onion and coriander, then place in a mixing bowl along with the lime zest and juice, Super Sauce, minced garlic and black pepper.

Roast the sweet peppers, ideally over the gas burners on your stove top. A similar effect can be achieved with electric rings or a very hot grill. Turn the peppers to blacken the skin across all sides. Set them aside to cool before finely chopping and adding the roasted peppers to the mixing bowl.

Skin the mangos with a potato peeler and remove the flesh from the stones in the largest chunks you can manage.

Heat the oil in a good quality non-stick frying pan or sauté pan and fry the mango until the pieces have a deep brown caramelisation on each side. Remove them from the pan and allow to cool. Finely chop and add the caramelised mango to the mixing bowl.

Mix all the ingredients together well and add salt to taste. Don't skimp on the salt; it works well with the sweet and citrus flavours.

Serve in corn tortillas with our Chilli and Lime Mexican Pork Shoulder, or with any of your other favourite Mexican dishes.

SPICED HOT CHOCOLATE

Preparation time: 5 minutes | Cooking time: 10 minutes | Serves 4

Fatalii and Lemon Aji chillies in our Golden Syrup pair perfectly with dark chocolate to create a truly decadent tipple that's rich and velvety with enough fiery notes to really warm the cockles. Any 50% cocoa chocolate is suitable. We sourced ours as handy drinking-chocolate buttons from Cocoa Wonderland on Ecclesall Road.

1 Madagascan vanilla pod
1 large cinnamon stick
Seeds of 6 green cardamon pods
Pinch of black pepper
Pinch of sea salt
700ml full fat milk
110g 50-60% cocoa dark chocolate
4 tsp Khoo's Golden Syrup, or to taste
1 cup of hot water (optional)

To serve
4 cinnamon sticks
Pinch of grated chocolate

Coarsely chop the vanilla pod. Place in a pan with the rest of the spices, salt and milk. Bring to a gentle simmer for 15 minutes.

Use a sieve to strain the milk and discard the spices. Return the spiced milk to the pan and add the dark chocolate. Bring back to a gentle simmer and stir until the chocolate has melted completely.

Add the Khoo's Golden Syrup, stir well and taste. This recipe makes a very rich cup of hot chocolate, so if you'd like to tone it down a notch, add some hot water to suit your taste.

Serve with a cinnamon stick stirrer and garnish with the grated chocolate.

COCOA
WONDERLAND
proper
hot chocolate
KEO'S
HOT SAUCE

LOVING LOCAL

A community store selling goods from a wide variety of local producers, Knab Farm Shop proudly flies the flag for all things made in Sheffield...

You'll find Knab Farm Shop situated on Montrose Road, part of a long-established small parade of shops between Millhouses and Carter Knowle. Co-owners Ian Proctor and Mary Tyas took over the reins in August 2021 with the aim of continuing to serve the local community whilst also bringing a wider mix of local producers into the fold, thereby creating a welcoming hub for supporting independent businesses across the region.

The shop still ticks all the boxes as a neighborhood stop-off to pick up essentials, but you can also browse wares from over 50 artisan producers, showcasing everything from wines and cakes to eco-friendly flowers and candles. A popular offering is the restaurant-quality ready meals sourced directly from the kitchens of Sheffield culinary gems, meaning customers can pick up an expertly prepared Bhaji Shop curry or an Italian dish from Marco at Milano to enjoy in the comfort of their homes.

"We want to be the home for Sheffield-produced food," says Ian. "But food and drink aren't the only focus here; we stock artisan products from the likes of Sheffield Candle Company, lip balms from Smallwood Bees and organic soaps from Chaar Soap Co. We're here to provide a strong local alternative to packaged goods from big supermarkets, a place where people can explore a wide range of independent producers who are part of the fabric of this city."

A key part of the Knab ethos is a commitment to promoting small start-ups, which means they became the first retail outlet stocking the likes of Nevertheless Cakes and The Heart of Sicily - two businesses run by young Sheffield-based entrepreneurs, who continue to supply their goods to the farm shop. Another important aspect is sustainability, clearly spelt out in a commitment to reducing food miles but also evidenced by the refill stations and various zero-waste products you'll find inside.

Moving forward, they will launch The Sheffield Hamper Company where you'll be able to receive a special selection of Sheffield-made products with a specific theme. That could be a wellness themed 'Take Care of Thisen' hamper with teas, soaps, honey and candles inside, or a 'Sheffield Spice' sweet box containing a variety of tasty treats to get stuck into. Naturally, there'll be a 'Homage to Hendo's" hamper on offer and a 'Full Monty' special if you're looking to go the whole way with a wider selection of products.

In a world where shopping local has never been more important, Knab Farm Shop provides a small haven for Sheffield producers to connect with consumers in their city. It's perhaps best summed up by Ian's go-to motto: "Let's get vocal about local."

Knab Farm
Shop

Knab
Farm Shop

£1.95/kg
Red onion £1.80/Kg
White onion £1.60/Kg

£3.10/kg
Braeburn £3.10/Kg
Pink lady

LEMON AND GINGER BAKED CHEESECAKE

Preparation time: 20 minutes, plus chilling | Cooking time: 50-55 minutes | Serves 8

This cheesecake was inspired by some of the many ingredients in Knab Farm Shop, and Ian's favourite dessert! The fruit on the top can be changed with the season, but we think that raspberries and blueberries work well with lemon and ginger.

For the base

250g good quality ginger biscuits, smashed into crumbs

100g butter, melted

For the filling

680g mascarpone cheese

100g caster sugar

2 eggs

70g Greek style yoghurt

1 lemon, zested

For the topping

5 heaped tbsp lemon curd

500g raspberries/blueberries/blackberries

Preheat the oven to 200°c or gas mark 6. Line a 20cm baking tin.

Combine the crushed biscuits and melted butter in a large bowl. Tip this mixture into the tin and use a spoon to carefully press the crumb mixture evenly to form a base. Place in the fridge to set while preparing the filling.

Beat the mascarpone cheese and sugar together in a large bowl until light and fluffy. Add the eggs and beat until fully incorporated, then stir in the yoghurt and lemon zest.

Remove the chilled base from the fridge and pour the filling into the tin. Bake in the preheated oven for 45-55 minutes (reducing the temperature slightly towards the end of cooking if it starts to colour too much), or until the cheesecake is just set. Turn off the oven, leave the door open and leave the cheesecake in the oven for a further hour.

When cool, place the baked cheesecake in the fridge to chill, ideally overnight. In the morning, gently spread the lemon curd onto the surface of the cheesecake, then return it to the fridge for at least 2 hours. Decorate with the fresh fruit just before serving.

For a variation on this recipe, replace the lemon zest with orange zest, use orange curd and top with clementine segments.

CELEBRATING EVERYTHING SOCIAL

Established in 2018, Kommune is a take on the future of social spaces, a place where an eclectic community of people choose to eat, drink and play; a place of serendipitous meeting; a place for ideas and great coffee to percolate; a place for everyone to share and enjoy.

Food is at the heart of social interaction and the aim has always been to celebrate that notion, working hard to curate an evolving blend of traders, from local chefs just starting out to street food vendors looking for a permanent home, bringing together new flavours and old favourites to treat everyone's tastebuds.

The raw concrete and great bones of the refurbished iconic, listed Co-op building Kommune calls home are complemented by eight open kitchens, two bars, a deli, a renowned independent beer shop and a specialist coffee shop. Together they bring a world of food and drink to the customer, including regional Vietnamese noodles by Hanoi 75, Mexican and Indian street food from Mucha Lucha and Chaat Cart, authentic Greek gyros from Greek Village, mouthwatering Korean fried chicken from Yoki and 'good old fashioned, roll up your sleeves and get it all over your face' burgers from Fat Hippo.

Drinks at the two bars are created to complement the flavours of the kitchens through serving a great selections of beers, wine and cocktails, whilst La Biblioteka – the coolest indie bookstore in town – serves up an amazing array of specialist magazines and books. A fully-packed music, exhibition, market and events programme across the venue sets the vibe day and night.

Kommune is a key element in bringing Sheffield's landmark Castle House back into use as a vibrant meeting place, forming part of a wider goal to transform not only this significant building but act as a catalyst for the regeneration of the historic Castlegate area of the city centre, which is the birthpalce of the city.

Rewarded with great national reviews including featuring in the Guardian and Waitrose Good Food Magazine, Kommune has become recognised as a destination, not just for locals, but also national and international visitors to our city.

KOMMUNE

LA BIBLIOTEKA

HANOI 75'S VIETNAMESE STIR FRIED NOODLES

Preparation time: 20 minutes | Cooking time: 15 minutes | Serves 2

A street food favourite in Hanoi and the stir fried version of the infamous pho noodle soup, our combination of flavours and spices is a heady example of the vibrancy Vietnamese cuisine can offer. This is one of our most popular dishes from over the years, paired with steak, crispy tofu and grilled chicken. The freshness of the coriander and the saltiness of our homemade sauce makes this more than a regular stir fry.

For the sauce
450ml boiling water
1 vegetable stock cube
125g dark brown sugar
15g fresh garlic
7g fresh ginger
250ml light soy sauce
10ml rice wine vinegar
5ml sesame oil
30g cornflour

For the noodles and vegetables
200g rice noodles
1 white onion, cut into thin slices
1 red pepper, cut into thin strips
1 tomato, cut into wedges
Handful of spinach

For the garnish
Drizzle of garlic and chilli sriracha
Drizzle of sweet soy sauce
Pinch of fresh coriander
Sprinkle of crushed peanuts
Sprinkle of crispy fried shallots
1 fresh red chilli, finely sliced

For the sauce

Pour the boiling water into a large mixing bowl, add the vegetable stock cube and mix until dissolved, then stir in the dark brown sugar.

In a food blender, combine the garlic and ginger with splash of water and blend until they form a paste. Combine this with the sweetened stock.

Add the light soy, rice wine vinegar and sesame oil to the bowl. Finally, mix the cornflour with a little water until dissolved, then add it to the bowl and stir until combined.

For the noodles and vegetables

Bring a pan of water to a slight simmer, add the noodles and cook on a medium heat for 2-5 minutes until barely tender. Drain and then rinse with cold water to stop them cooking.

Add a tablespoon of oil to a frying pan or wok and cook the onions and peppers until slightly soft. Next, add the tomatoes and then mix in your sauce. Cook until it goes slightly sticky, then add your cooked noodles and mix well. Once the noodles are almost cooked and piping hot, add the spinach and cook until wilted.

To serve

Divide the noodle mixture between bowls, then add a drizzle of garlic sriracha and sweet soy, a pinch of crushed peanuts, crispy shallots and fresh coriander, and some fresh red chillies to taste. Enjoy.

YEE KWAN'S BANGKOK BELLE MOCHI WAFFLE

Preparation time: 20 minutes | Cooking time: 5 minutes | Serves 1-2

I've always had a fascination with Japan, and my trip to Tokyo in 2018 inspired our "Maffles" (mochi waffles) and Harajuku crepe cones on the menu.

3 eggs
1050ml whole milk
2g vanilla paste
685g plain flour
75g glutinous rice flour
75g sugar
20g cornflour
15g baking powder
1g salt

To serve
Ice cream
Fresh mango
Passionfruit sauce
Toasted coconut sprinkles

Beat the eggs until frothy, then add the milk and vanilla paste and beat for 1 minute.
Weigh the dry ingredients into a bowl and stir well until mixed.
Add the wet ingredients into the dry ingredients and mix for 20 seconds until smooth. DO NOT over mix or they will become chewy and tough.
Let the mixture rest for at least 10 minutes in the fridge prior to using.
Meanwhile, lightly spray the waffle irons with oil to ensure the batter doesn't stick, then set the temperature of the waffle iron to 150°c and leave it to warm up.
Pour the batter onto the bottom plate (you should need 120ml of mixture per portion) and carefully close the waffle iron. Set a timer for 2 minutes.
Make sure the waffle is golden brown and then remove using tongs and place on a cooling rack. Repeat to use up all the batter.

To serve
Put the waffles onto a plate, scoop some ice cream on the centre of the waffles and add some fresh mango cubes, lashings of passionfruit sauce, and decorate with fragrant toasted coconut. Sprinkle with icing sugar and enjoy!

KOMMUNE BAR'S PORNSTAR MARTINI

Preparation time: 2 minutes | Serves 1

Whether you love a Pornstar Martini or not, it is a perennial favourite in Kommune. Everyone has tried one (or more) so being a place for everyone, we thought we'd share how we do it, so you can try one at home.

37.5ml vanilla vodka
25ml passionfruit liqueur
50ml pineapple juice
12.5ml sugar syrup
25ml lime juice
25ml Prosecco
Ice
1 passionfruit, halved

Start by filling a quarter of the boston glass with ice. Pour in all of the ingredients except the Prosecco. Close the boston glass with the top part and give it a tap with your palm to make sure it is securely closed. Shake it well for at least 10 seconds. Remove the top by tapping on the side of the glass. Place the cocktail strainer onto the boston and start pouring into the coupe glass through the sieve. Wait 10 seconds for the cocktail to settle and form a layer of foam.

To serve
Slowly place one half of the passionfruit on top of the foam. Pour the Prosecco into shot glass and and your cocktail is ready to serve. Cheers!

MUCHA LUCHA'S BEEF BRISKET TACOS

Preparation time: 20 minutes, plus marinating overnight | Cooking time: 8 hours | Serves 4-6

This accessible take on a classic Northern Mexican barbacoa uses beef in place of goat or mutton and locally sourced chillies, but we encourage you to experiment with exotic dried chillies from Sheffield's various suppliers if you want to dive deeper into authentic Mexican cuisine! Recipe adapted from Scott Drury.

5 x 10-15cm medium heat fresh chillies (such as serrano)
½ large bulb of garlic
100ml white wine vinegar
100ml lime juice
1 tbsp ground cumin
1 tbsp smoked paprika
1 tbsp dried oregano
5 cloves
Salt, to taste
1.25kg beef brisket
1 beef stock cube
Corn or flour tortillas

Prepare your chillies and garlic for the marinade: remove the tops from the chillies and roughly chop, and peel and roughly chop the garlic.

Add the chillies, garlic, white wine vinegar, lime juice, dry spices and herbs to a blender. Blitz until smooth. Add salt to taste.

Place the beef brisket in a large ovenproof dish. Salt liberally. Add the marinade, cover, and leave to marinate at least overnight and for up to 48 hours.

Preheat the oven to 180°c. Rehydrate a beef stock cube and pour the stock over the beef until the meat is fully submerged. Cover and cook in the oven for 6-8 hours. When done, you should be able to shred the beef very easily with a fork. Remove from the oven and shred the meat.

Carefully strain the cooking liquids into a heavy-bottomed pot. Reduce on a low heat for about an hour, or until the liquid is one third to one quarter of its initial volume. Pour this over the beef.

Serve the beef in corn or flour tortillas with accompaniments of your choice! We like to serve this in portions of 3 tacos per person with caramelised onions, roast peppers, salsas, house pickles, coriander, and lime.

FAST FOOD, BUT NOT AS YOU KNOW IT

Currently based in Cutlery Works but soon to move into its own premises, Konjö is an Eastern Asian inspired hotspot with an irresistible menu of top-quality fast food.

The driving force behind Konjö is food that the owners and chefs love to eat. Inspired by Eastern Asian favourites including katsu curry, bao, Korean fried chicken, donburi and more, the eatery uses incredible ingredients to create fast food like no other. Konjö is the little sister of JÖRO, one of Sheffield's most acclaimed restaurants by Luke French and Stacey Sherwood-French.

The pair initially began discussing the idea of opening a second venue because they wanted somewhere to enjoy the Asian flavours they loved on their days off, but realised that it could also provide an outlet for the excess produce that comes with fine dining, particularly from buying in whole animals. Stacey came up with a name – the first halves of konro, a Japanese barbecue, and JÖRO – and they soon joined up the dots to trial their casual dining venture at Cutlery Works, a popular food hall in Neepsend, in late 2019.

The combination of traditional fast food favourites, top quality ingredients and chefs from within the JÖRO team ensured that Konjö was a hit from the get go. Luke created the initial menu but gave his team free rein to put their own twist on the food, drawing on original recipes and ingredients from JÖRO's kitchen to develop the signature dishes like Korean Fried Chicken. Today, the offering at Konjö changes seasonally and is defined by the restaurant's by-products which not only makes both venues more efficient but ensures an amazing standard of ingredients.

Crispy chilli beef, donburi and bao are just a few of the staple dishes on the menu. These are elevated to deliver complex flavours and allow people to customise their food, for example with a choice of sauces, seasonings and toppings on the Korean Fried Chicken. Following the move upstairs to occupy a larger kitchen space within Cutlery Works, Konjö will move into its own venue during 2023, allowing Luke and Stacey to have full control of the environment and build on their burgeoning success. Head chef Joel Darby and his right-hand man, Joshua Green, who both progressed through the kitchen at JÖRO, will also take their expertise into Konjö's new setting.

"It's really important to us that we're promoting from within the group," explains Luke. "We have a tight-knit family unit here which helps everyone to understand the ethos and share our vision."

KONJÖ

CHICKEN KATSU BAO

Preparation time: 30 minutes, plus 24 hours marinating | Cooking time: 20-30 minutes | Serves 4

Stacey & I are obsessed with bao: little pockets of savoury-sweet filled goodies. You can pretty much put anything you want into them and they're mega! This one is filled with our take on traditional chicken katsu curry, full of texture, full of flavour and absolutely delicious!

For the marinade
150g each vegetable oil & sake
25g soy sauce
6g each sesame oil & salt
200g buttermilk

For the chicken
4 boneless chicken thighs
60g self-raising flour
35g cornflour
30g potato flour
Curry powder, salt and sugar

For the curry ketchup
240g caster sugar
150g chicken stock
90g rice wine vinegar
60g fermented rice
60g mirin
7.5g madras blend
7.5g onion powder
6g garlic powder
4.8g agar agar
4.5g turmeric
2g masala blend
0.5g MSG

To serve
4 bao buns
Katsu curry sauce

For the brine
Combine all the ingredients and blend together using a hand blender. Pour the brine over the prepared chicken thighs and drumsticks, then chill for 24 hours.

For the dredging mix
Combine all the ingredients in a bowl and whisk together, then reserve in an airtight container.

For the sauce
Place the soy sauce, mirin, apple juice, sake and sesame oil in a saucepan. Bring to the boil, then transfer to a high-powered blender and blend in all the remaining ingredients except the gochujang and miso. Once combined, add these last ingredients and blend in, then pass the sauce through a sieve and let it cool.

To prepare and cook the chicken
Heat a deep pan of cooking oil to 160°c. Remove the chicken from the brine and dredge it through the flour mix 2-3 times so it is well coated. Deep fry the coated chicken carefully until the core temperature reaches 75°c. If you do not have a temperature probe, the chicken should feel piping hot in the centre and the juices should run clear.

Heat the sauce up, just to warm it. Allow the chicken to cool down slightly and then toss the chicken in the warm sauce, making sure it is coated all over.

Serve with some freshly chopped spring onion, coriander and sesame seeds sprinkled over it.

KOREAN FRIED CHICKEN

Preparation time: 30 minutes, plus 24 hours brining | Cooking time: 1 hour 30 minutes | Serves 4

We serve a few different types of fried chicken, but this is our signature fried chicken at KONJÖ. We have taken a classic Korean fried chicken recipe and developed it further with the brine and some of the epic Japanese ingredients we use in our kitchens.

2 corn-fed free-range chicken legs, cut into thighs and drumsticks

For the brine

50g each vegetable oil, buttermilk, sake and light soy sauce

10g each golden roasted sesame oil and caster sugar

5g MSG

For the dredging mix

200g each self-raising and potato flour

100g cornflour, 30g table salt

For the sauce

75g light soy sauce, 60g hon mirin

50g each sour apple juice and brown rice sake

10g golden roasted sesame oil

100g dark muscovado sugar

50ml rice wine vinegar

3 cloves of garlic, peeled and chopped

2 spring onions, chopped

1 tbsp freshly chopped coriander

1 tsp fresh root ginger, peeled and diced

1 tsp Chinese chicken granules

50g each gochujang paste & chilli miso

To serve

Spring onions, coriander & sesame seeds

Finely chop the onion and coriander, then place in a mixing bowl along with the lime zest and juice, Super Sauce, minced garlic and black pepper.

Roast the sweet peppers, ideally over the gas burners on your stove top. A similar effect can be achieved with electric rings or a very hot grill. Turn the peppers to blacken the skin across all sides. Set them aside to cool before finely chopping and adding the roasted peppers to the mixing bowl.

Skin the mangos with a potato peeler and remove the flesh from the stones in the largest chunks you can manage.

Heat the oil in a good quality non-stick frying pan or sauté pan and fry the mango until the pieces have a deep brown caramelisation on each side. Remove them from the pan and allow to cool. Finely chop and add the caramelised mango to the mixing bowl.

Mix all the ingredients together well and add salt to taste. Don't skimp on the salt; it works well with the sweet and citrus flavours.

Serve in corn tortillas with our Chilli and Lime Mexican Pork Shoulder, or with any of your other favourite Mexican dishes.

CRISPY SHREDDED CHILLI BEEF

Preparation time: 12 hours | Cooking time: 1 hour | Serves 4

This is our all-time favourite Chinese takeaway dish and the first dish we developed for KONJÖ, slightly tweaked for the home cook. We first set up KONJÖ so that we (Stacey & I, and the JÖRO team) had somewhere undeniably delicious to eat on our days off!

For the brined beef

50g each barley miso, Chinese rice wine, mirin and shio koji

400g Wortley wagyu short-rib meat

For the sauce

300g Bramley apple juice

300g caster sugar

150g shio koji

100g each tadokoro chilli miso and white miso

60g mirin

40g each white soy sauce and light soy sauce

20g yuzu juice

8 cloves of garlic, microplaned

30g fresh ginger, microplaned

For the dredge

60g self-raising flour

30g each cornflour and potato flour

5g crytex

2g table salt

To cook the beef

2 litres vegetable/cooking oil

To garnish

1 lime, zested

1-2 red chillies, finely sliced

For the brined beef

Combine everything except the beef and bring to the boil, then chill. Pour over the beef and leave to marinate for 12 hours in the fridge. Strain off the brine and pat the beef dry, then leave to air dry in the fridge until needed.

For the sauce

Place everything into a saucepan and slowly bring to the boil. Simmer for 10 minutes, then blend together and reserve until needed.

For the dredge

Place everything in a bowl and whisk together. Keep in an airtight tub until needed.

To cook the beef

Heat the oil to 180°c in a heavy-based saucepan. Coat the brined and air dried beef in the dredge mixture and leave it to absorb it for 5 minutes. Shake the beef in a colander or sieve to remove any excess dredge. Deep fry the beef in small batches until it is dark brown in colour and crispy. This will take approximately 3-5 minutes depending on how much you fry at once. Remove from the oil and drain on kitchen paper.

To serve

Toss the beef through the sauce (using just enough sauce to coat the beef well) then arrange it in a serving dish and garnish with the fresh lime zest and shredded red chilli.

TASTY IN LATIN

A stalwart of the Abbeydale Road food scene, La Mama is a well-reputed gem when it comes to bringing a taste of Latin America to the Steel City.

Opening its doors in 2009, the award-winning tapas hotspot has stood the test of time by serving up a truly authentic experience in a cosy, welcoming setting. Owner Daniela Cooke is of Chilean heritage and named the restaurant in tribute to her abuela (grandmother) and mama (mother), whose recipes have been lovingly passed down through the family, helping to lay the foundations for a unique menu bursting with standout Latino flavours.

The intimate restaurant seats 35-40 diners at a push, but what the venue may lack in size, it more than makes up for in character. It's a vibrant, colourful space that reflects the warmth exuded by their small, dedicated team; you'll find the walls adorned with photographs taken by Daniela while travelling across South America, further complemented by artworks of famous historical figures from the continent and an eye-catching painting of the renowned cartoon character 'Condorita', hand-painted by a Chilean artist.

Pick up a menu and you'll see what they're about: bold, uncompromising flavours and family favourites passed through the generations, sometimes tweaked by head chef Andy Sanderson to keep things fresh and exciting. Authenticity is at the heart of the La Mama philosophy; they source everything from organic Columbian panela sugar right through to the cranberry beans used in traditional countryside stews. They even offer two craft beers – an IPA and Golden Ale – made by independent Chilean brewery Rotherhammer, one of few restaurants in the country to do so.

Over the years La Mama has built up a dedicated following in Sheffield, forming longstanding relationships with customers while always keen to embrace new friends. Daniela tells us that some dishes have been so successful from day one, they've never left! The Chilean Sopaipillas have been one such mainstay, a delightful street food staple of lightly fried pumpkin bread served with tangy salsa pebre. Another well-established favourite is their famous Porotos Verdes dish, which regularly has diners puzzled as to how so much flavour can come from green beans!

That said, the menu does change seasonally and they continue to add to their offering. A popular recent addition has been the Brunch Sin Fondo, an afternoon bottomless brunch of tasty arepas options served with a selection of drinks including a special Chilean espresso martini. Head on down and raise a glass to some of the finest tapas you'll find in these seven hills!

LaMama
Latin Tapas Bar & Restaurant

SOPAIPILLAS AND PEBRE

Preparation time: 2-3 hours | Cooking time: 30 minutes | Serves 4-6

Chilean sopaipillas are a delightful street food made of fried pumpkin dough which is served with pebre, a Chilean chopped salsa. Sopaipillas are a delicious part of the heritage of Chilean cuisine and were one of the first things I learnt to make as a child with my Mami Norma (grandmother).

For the pebre

150g tomato, diced
150g red onion, diced
200g fresh coriander, chopped
1 or 2 chilies, finely chopped
1 tsp minced garlic
1 tbsp olive oil
1 tbsp lime juice
Salt and black pepper, to taste

For the sopaipillas

1 butternut squash
200g flour
¼ tsp salt
2 tbsp warm vegetable oil
600ml vegetable oil, for frying

For the pebre

Pebre is best made a few hours before serving, to let the flavours come together. All the ingredients can be chopped very small by hand. We prefer to use a food processor to make it a little runnier and finer but you can choose your own method. Combine all the ingredients in a medium-size bowl. Cover and place in the refrigerator until you're ready to use. Pebre is best eaten the day it is made.

For the sopaipillas

Bring a big saucepan of water to the boil and chop the butternut squash into large pieces. Boil the squash until tender, about 15 minutes, then set the squash on a clean surface and scoop out the flesh. Mash it with a fork.

In a large bowl, combine the flour, salt, and mashed squash. Add the warm oil (making sure it's not too hot) and mix until the dough comes together. Knead the dough for 3-5 minutes with your hands. Cover and let it rest for 10 minutes.

Divide the rested dough into 8 equal portions and shape each piece into a smooth ball. Cover and let them rest for 5 minutes.

Flatten each sopaipilla with your hands or use a rolling pin until they are ¼ inch thick. Prick with a fork. Heat the oil on medium-low, until hot but not smoking. Fry 2 or 3 sopaipillas at a time for 1-2 minutes on each side, or until golden brown. Transfer the fried sopaipillas to a baking sheet lined with paper towels to drain and cool slightly. Serve with the pebre.

LE'GIN'DARY LOCKSLEY DISTILLING

Locksley Distilling's small but passionate team have been bringing the unexpected to the spirits world since 2013. Never happy to give you a tipple that you can find elsewhere, the team thrives on finding a unique twist to make all their products quirky and memorable.

In early 2013, John Cherry and Cynthia King stepped off a plane from NYC and started Locksley Distilling Co. Ltd in John's parents' house in Sheffield. What began as one person in an attic has grown into a team of ten, operating from their distillery in Portland Works, a Grade II* listed building.

Sir Robin of Locksley Distilled Artisan Gin was Locksley's first and flagship product. When it launched, there was nothing else like it on the market: a smooth sipping gin that needs no mixer (though it is gorgeous in a G&T). The qualities and values that made them stand out from their inception continue to set them apart in an increasingly competitive crowd.

When pink gins exploded onto the scene, John resisted, not wanting to follow the trend. His wife, Cynthia, snuck behind his back trying different flavour combinations until she hit on something that she absolutely loved. The Real Raspberry and Cardamom version was born, once again surprising the ginthusiastic palate with a savoury, almost dry gin, hidden in what appears to be something sweet.

The third of the core range is another product that has never been done before; John had the brilliant idea to combine two old styles of gin together in one bottle. Their VSOT is the first ever Navy Strength Old Tom, in which the sweetness and strength balance each other perfectly, making it an ideal cocktail ingredient.

Locksley are not just gin makers, they make a range of liqueurs that bring unique flavours to cocktails and mixed drinks, and are developing an absinthe, an amaro, and a few other spirits.

The newest range, The Co-Lab, is the one that makes the team proudest, highlighting Locksley's collaborative and innovative side. To date, the team has created 14 collaborative products (with at least another five in development) with other local producers, restaurants, and even the Crucible Theatre. Cynthia says: "We love brainstorming flavour possibilities with our Co-Lab partners; it is so satisfying when we are able to deliver exactly what they want."

"There is nothing more rewarding than sharing our love and passion for the products we create through events, gin schools, master classes, and tastings so that others can enjoy or be inspired by our journey," adds John Cherry, the company's founder, MD, and Head Distiller. All products are created, distilled, bottled, and packed at their distillery in Sheffield.

CO-LAB

LIMITED
VODKA
A.B.V (%): 40.0
Batch/Bottle
CO-LAB
BULLION
CRAFT CHOCOLATE
DISTILLED COCOA NIB LIQUEUR
ORIGIN: PERU, UCAVALI RIVER
2021 HARVEST
A.B.V (%):
Batch/Bottle:
LIMITED
VODKA
Madagascan Vanilla
CO-LAB
FOUNDRY COFFEE ROASTERS
DISTILLED SPECIALITY COFFEE LIQUEUR
SINGLE ORIGIN COFFEE - 2021 HARVEST
YIRGACHEFFE - ETHIOPIA
Method:
Vacuum distilled
A.B.V (%):
27%

CRYSTAL CLEAR MOCHA MARTINI

Preparation time: less than 5 minutes | Makes 1 cocktail (can easily be multiplied)

An elegant version of the ever-popular Espresso Martini, our crystal-clear version has no caffeine, but is still full of mocha flavour. A surprise in a glass; it needs to be tried to be believed.

50ml Co-Lab cocoa nib liqueur
37.5ml Co-Lab coffee liqueur
25ml vodka
5ml vanilla vodka

Add all the ingredients to a mixing glass and then fill with ice. Stir gently for 30-45 seconds, until the drink is chilled and diluted, and then strain into a pre-chilled martini glass. Finally, garnish with three coffee beans – these represent health, happiness, and prosperity.

CHOCOLATE RASPBERRY NEGRONI

Looking for other ways to use the coffee and cocoa nib Co-Labs? Either can be stirred into some classic cocktails. We love the cocoa nib liqueur in this Chocolate Raspberry Negroni, and the coffee gives a gorgeous background note to an Old Fashioned.

50ml Sir Robin of Locksley raspberry and cardamom gin
25ml Co-Lab cocoa nib liqueur
20ml Campari
25ml high quality sweet vermouth
5ml fig liqueur (optional, for added complexity)

Add all the ingredients to a mixing glass and then fill with ice. Stir gently for 30-45 seconds, until the drink is chilled and diluted, and then strain into an old-fashioned glass over a large block of ice. For an extra special serve, see our Instagram page for a tutorial on slanted ice.

VODKA

MEDITERRANEAN SUNSHINE IN THE STEEL CITY

All about good food and good wine, Luca is a restaurant bringing some Mediterranean flair to Sheffield.

Luca opened in October 2021, transforming a bar and grill into a neighbourhood restaurant in Oughtibridge. The venue boasts a grill and a Mediterranean feel, building on the previous incarnation that customers were familiar with. This has been coupled with a complete overhaul of the interior to create a cosy and welcoming space with a hint of taverna in the décor.

Overseen by executive chef Richard Barber, the head chef designs Luca's menu in collaboration with his small team, as the managers are keen for individuals to contribute as much as possible. They have free rein to create whatever dishes work for Luca's seasonal menu, utilising the grill and double pizza oven to their full potential. Favourites include the beef shin rigatoni, which features a ragu cooked for six to seven hours and has been a hit with customers right from day one.

Local produce is an important cornerstone of the restaurant group's ethos, so they aim to use the same suppliers for all three sites such as their veg supplier in Barnsley. Luca also uses John Crawshaws, a butchers just down the road in Hillsborough, while Gaard uses vegan ingredients to show people just how tasty plant-based food can be and Joni is renowned for excellent coffee. It all comes down to attention to detail, from the coffee beans to the equipment, ensuring that the group can go above and beyond with the food and drink they deliver.

The newest addition of a second Joni, which opened in the summer of 2022 at Abbeydale Industrial Hamlet, is tucked away is a peaceful spot that even Sheffielders may not have come across. Executive chef Richard is excited by the brand's ambitions and explains that "it's a massive team effort across all the sites. We want our staff to work for a growing company and get involved so we can keep pushing forward." Luca and Joni mark two have both got off to a great start and there is still more to come in future, so watch this space and don't miss a visit to Luca in the meantime!

Luca
Pizza & Grill

Luca
Pizza & Grill
T: 07543183869
WWW.LUCARESTAURANTS.CO.UK

BIRRA
PERONI

BEEF SHIN RIGATONI

Preparation time: 30 minutes | Cooking time: 4-5 hours | Serves 6

This hearty pasta dish is a Luca favourite. Slow cooking, beautiful aromas, warming and perfect for al fresco dining or those cold winter months!

2 tbsp olive oil

750g-1kg beef shin (speak to your local butcher)

2 large onions, 1 cut into large chunks and the other finely diced

3 carrots, 1 into large chunks and the other finely diced

1 head of celery, ½ into large chunks and the other finely diced

6 cloves of garlic, ½ roughly chopped and the other half minced

150ml Henderson's Relish

2 litres beef stock

1 bunch of fresh thyme

1 bunch of fresh rosemary

2 tins of chopped tomatoes (or equivalent in passata)

1 bunch of basil, stalks finely chopped and leaves thinly sliced

500g dried rigatoni pasta

Salt and black pepper

In a cast iron casserole dish or ovenproof pan, heat up the oil. Season the shin generously and colour the meat, then remove from the pan and set aside. Fry the roughly chopped veg and garlic to get colour on them, then de-glaze the pan with half of the Henderson's Relish and add the beef stock. Place the shin back into the pan and bring to the boil. Add the thyme and rosemary, then place in a preheated oven at 140°c and cook for about 3 hours or until the shin falls away from the bone.
When the meat is ready, sauté the rest of the finely diced veg in a separate pan until soft and a little coloured. Strain the beef shin cooking liquor and pour half of this into the sautéed veg, reserving the rest to loosen the sauce later if needed. Reduce the volume by half, then add the tomatoes and chopped basil stalks and simmer until the sauce is rich and reduced, about 20 minutes.
Shred the meat, removing any sinew, and add it to the tomato sauce. Check and adjust the seasoning. Cook the pasta in a pan of boiling, very well salted water (my mentor Antonio Carluccio would say like the sea!) for 8 minutes. Drain and stir into the sauce, cooking the pasta for the final minute or so. Add the sliced basil leaves and, if needed, a little of the reserved stock to loosen the sauce. Pile high in a bowl, then finish with grated parmesan and a little fresh rocket.

WHAT A LOT OF BOTTLE!

Mitchells Wine Merchants is an integral part of Sheffield's retail community, and their name has been known in Meadowhead for over 85 years.

This renowned departmental store is run by Frankie Mitchell – the third generation of the family to do so – and her husband James. Mitchells Wine Merchants are highly regarded throughout Yorkshire, winning a huge number of awards including Wine Merchant of the Year twice. The heavily stocked cabinets feature 1000+ whiskeys from around the world, from your everyday drinking bottle to the best of the best, limited editions and collectables. Being a departmental store means the fridges are lined with 1000+ beers, including craft brews, English bottled ales and ready chilled world beers with a special focus on those from Germany.

Throw in vodkas, rums, gins, Cognacs, Armagnacs and brandies, cocktails, tequilas, liqueurs and aperitifs, and you've almost covered their offering! Mitchells also holds an impressive selection of Havana cigars; spread over five fabulous humidors, they stand as the second largest specialist retailer of Havanas in the north. But it's not just about the Havanas, their selection now includes over 200 new world cigars from some of the world's most sought-after producers.

Wines and champagnes are very much at the forefront of the store, with over 2500 from all around the world and a key focus on diversity, while refreshing the selection all the time and keeping up with trends including quality non-alcoholic, natural unfiltered, and orange wines. If there is something new that you're looking for but not quite sure, their 16-bottle Enomatic wine machines facilitate the option to freely try before you buy, encouraging customers to step outside comfort zones and expand palates.

Mitchells also has a specialised tasting room and museum holding memorabilia collected over the last 50 years. The tasting room itself holds 35 people, and Mitchells run two or three tasting events every month. With whisky and cigar tastings by far being the most popular, they bring in distillers, producers and ambassadors from all around the UK and across the globe.

From starting as a small family business to delivering far and wide, Mitchells continues to achieve. Sending out orders both locally and nationally, they have made it easier for everyone to try their products, bringing the fun straight to your doorstep. With such an illustrious history and unique array of products, their place in Sheffield is firmly secured, and manager Frankie hopes that the family will continue to bring some of life's biggest pleasures to the city for many more generations to come. Mitchells would like to thank you all for your continued loyalty, supporting local independents and keeping Sheffield's scene thriving.

SPEYSIDE
HIGHLANDS

EST 1935 IN SHEFFIELD
MITCHELLS WINES
EST 1935 IN SHEFFIELD

SPEYSIDE
HIGHLANDS
HIGHLANDS
CAMPBELTOWN
ISLANDS
GLENGOYNE
10
BENROMACH
SPEYSIDE
SINGLE MALT
SCOTCH
WHISKY
FORRES · SCOTLAND

WHISKY AND CIGARS

Here at Mitchells, we pride ourselves on the extensive range we offer. We are forever changing and expanding our selection to bring you the best of the best. Over the last couple of years, whisky and cigars have taken a central focus in store.

Historically, Mitchells has been a specialist retailer for the prestigious Cuban cigars and although we still very much are, we have now opened up our range. Adding several new humidors, we have been able to bring in over 200 new cigars from the likes of Davidoff, Rocky Patel, Perdomo, Ghurka, Padron and Drew Estate just to name a few. Alongside our new range, we now have available some great smoking accessories including humidors, cutters, and ashtrays for any cigar enthusiast.

For a long time, we have been offering tasting evenings in our private tasting room at the shop but recently we have launched our outdoor cigar tasting evenings at venues across Sheffield and Derbyshire. These evenings allow smokers new and old to come along and enjoy fabulous cigars they may have never tried before, meet producers and dig deeper into the world of cigars.

Whisky is a huge part of our store too; we have recently had a new whisky department built instore which enabled us to expand our world whiskey and Bourbon offering. For many years, we have had a widespread Scottish single malt selection. However, as we have seen people's tastes and interests change over time, we felt we wanted to expand our world whiskeys further. We have welcomed onto our shelves the likes of Pappy van Winkle, Weller, Blantons, Sullivans Cove and many harder to find bottles. Alongside these rarities we have also been able to expand our selection in general, offering more varieties from Sweden, Japan, Ireland and other whisky producing countries.

Next time you're passing, come on in and have a nosey: our Aladdin's cave has something for everyone!

MONTECRISTO
HAND MADE HAVANA CIGARS
Smoking clogs your arteries

ROMEO Y JULIETA
Desde 1875
HABANA · CUBA

ELIJAH CRAIG
1884
FEW

Littlemill
29
2019

The MACALLAN
The MACALLAN
25
The MACALLAN
30

LIKE A ROLLING STONE...

In 2007 Stephen and Karen Thompson finally had enough of selling their pigs to the big supermarkets for dire prices; it was time to take matters into their own hands.

That year they decided to make use of some pigs themselves for ham and bacon, and it went down an absolute storm! It was such a success that it gave them the idea to start their own butchery and, right there on Povey Farm soil, Moss Valley Fine Meats began.

Karen trained herself in the art of butchery but soon cottoned on that, where it was taking her a whole day to cut up a pig, a seasoned butcher could do it in twenty minutes. One butcher eventually became two, with the new team member bringing ideas like Tiger Tails (stuffed fillets wrapped in bacon). Moss Valley Meats has gone from having one butcher working a couple of hours a week, to three full-time members they now can't live without; the third being Lauren who's always on the lookout for new customers and fresh ideas, like new sausage varieties. Stephen, coming from a background as a fourth generation farmer at Povey, enjoys running the butchery and Karen rears the pigs. Their son Oliver, fifth generation, now runs the arable side and helps Karen with the livestock. It truly is a family affair.

Moss Valley Meats' bacon is always flying out in high demand. Bellies are also popular, especially with chefs, and shoulders do well too – Street Food Chef (another contributor in this book!) always orders plenty for their pulled pork burritos. For MVFM, attention to detail is key. The team is willing to go that extra mile for their customers, including supplying on Sundays, or cutting up meat orders in new ways for chefs. The beauty of using their own pigs is guaranteed consistency – if you like it once, you'll like it forever.

To keep the business sustainable and environmentally friendly, the team use fewer antibiotics than most farms – about 2% of what other pig farmers use – all through their biosecurity practices. They're also working hard to reduce their carbon footprint with a whole range of measures including: wind turbines, a straw burner, water borehole and solar photovoltaic panels. Their hard work is gaining the recognition it deserves, with multiple awards under their belt. Stephen's favourites include winning the first ever 'Made in Sheffield' award and the outstanding achievement award from the whole of the British pig industry.

Since opening, the business has quadrupled in size. Stephen and the team have plans in the pipeline to expand their services, including offering more outside catering. With sausage sandwiches already on the menu, look out for things like pot roasts, pulled pork, hot pies and more – all made with Moss Valley Meats' finest of course!

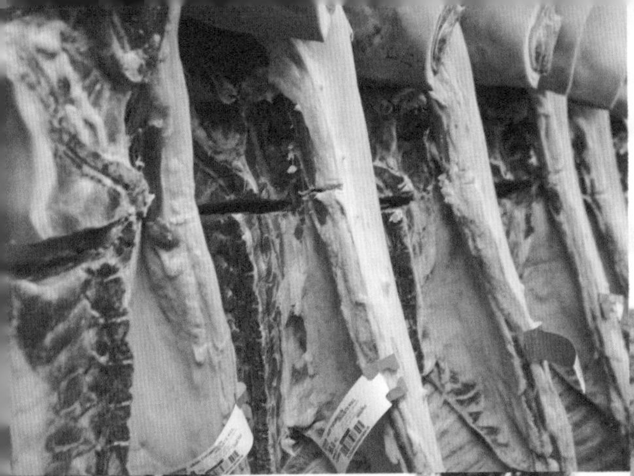

Moss Valley
Fine Meats
Naturally Different

HAM & EGG

Preparation time: 1 hour | Cooking time: 3-4 hours | Serves 4

This recipe was created by chef Mark Aisthorpe at The Bull's Head in Holymoorside, who are supplied by Moss Valley Fine Meats and use their top quality products to create delicious, refined yet hearty meals like this ham hock terrine starter with poached yolks and Henderson's Relish gel.

2 pig ham hocks from Moss Valley Fine Meats
1 onion, roughly chopped
2 cloves of garlic, crushed
A few sprigs of rosemary, thyme and sage, finely chopped
1 apple
35g shallot
10g parsley
10g capers
8g wholegrain mustard
100ml Henderson's relish
1-3g MSK UltraTex
4 eggs
4 slices of brioche bread
Micro parsley leaves and micro mustard frills (optional)
Truffle or 20g parmesan cheese

Place the hocks, onion, garlic, rosemary, thyme and sage into a pan with enough water to cover everything. Bring to the boil, then place a lid on and simmer for 3-4 hours until tender and falling to pieces.

Once cooked, drain the hocks and discard the liquid. Pull the meat apart using two forks – it should look something like pulled pork.

Finely dice the apple, shallot, parsley and capers. Combine these with the wholegrain mustard and mix into the shredded ham hock. Season to taste with salt and black pepper.

Lay a sheet of cling film on your work surface and place the ham hock mixture onto it. Roll tightly in the cling film to form a sausage shape and place in the fridge to set for 2-3 hours.

To make the Hendo's gel, simply place the relish in a bowl, sprinkle the UltraTex on top, then whisk to a ketchup consistency.

Separate the yolks from the whites of the eggs. Poach the yolks for 2-3 minutes, then carefully set them side ready to be served.

Meanwhile, toast the brioche and cut into fingers to serve on the side.

To serve

Slice the ham hock terrine into 4 discs and place one in each bowl. Pipe the Hendo's gel around the edge, reheat and sit the egg yolks in the middle, then arrange micro leaves around the yolk. Generously shave the truffle over the top or finish with ultra-finely grated parmesan.

PORK BELLY, GLAZED CARROT, MUSTARD MASH & APPLE SAUCE

Preparation time: 30-60 minutes | Cooking time: 5 hours | Serves 4-6

This recipe was created by chef Mark Aisthorpe at The Bull's Head in Holymoorside, who are supplied by Moss Valley Fine Meats and use their top quality products to create delicious, refined yet hearty meals like this pork belly with a rich sauce made from the cooking juices.

For the pork

4 onions (we use Roscoff)

1.2kg pork belly from Moss Valley Fine Meats

1 pint of cider

3 cloves of garlic

4 sprigs of sage and thyme

1 Jazz apple, chopped

For the carrots

4-6 carrots

150g butter

75g sugar

4 star anise

500ml water

A few chives, finely sliced

Handful of hazelnuts, toasted and chopped

For the mash

1kg potatoes (we use Yukon Gold)

Splash of milk & a knob of butter

Salt and pepper, to taste

1 tbsp wholegrain mustard

For the sauce

1 apple

200ml double cream

1 tbsp wholegrain mustard

For the pork

Preheat your oven to 200°c. Slice the onions in half, place in a roasting tray and pop them in the hot oven for about 10 minutes to get some colour. While the onion is roasting, allow the pork to come up to room temperature. Score the fat with a sharp knife in a crisscross pattern every 2mm, then pat dry and season heavily with sea salt. Place the pork on top of the browned onion and, without getting the skin wet, pour the cider into the tray and top up with enough water to reach just under the rind. Add the garlic, herbs and apple to the tray, then roast the pork for 45 minutes. After this time, turn the oven down to 170°c and roast for 4 hours until you have nice crackling on top and the pork underneath is soft.

For the glazed carrots

While the pork belly is cooking, peel the carrots until the tops are nice and round. Place all the ingredients, except the chives and hazelnuts, in a pan and bring to a simmer. Cook until the carrots are soft, then remove them from the liquid, leaving it in the pan. Brush the carrots with the buttery glaze and then roast for a few minutes to colour up nicely. Once ready to serve, sprinkle the glazed carrots with the chives and toasted hazelnuts.

For the mash

Peel the potatoes and cut into 2cm squares. Place in a pan and rinse with cold water for 5 minutes until it runs clear. Fill the pan with fresh water, add a good pinch of salt and boil for 20-25 minutes. Mash until smooth, then transfer to a stand mixer (like a KitchenAid or similar) with the whisk attachment. Add the milk, butter, salt and pepper, then whip for 5 minutes on full speed until smooth, light and airy. Add the wholegrain mustard and mix through to finish.

For the sauce

Strain the cooking liquid from the pork belly into a pan on a medium-high heat and reduce it by three quarters. Chop the apple into 1cm squares and place into the reduced liquid, then add the cream and boil down again until the sauce reaches a coating consistency. Stir in the mustard and then season to taste.

To serve

Cut the pork into 4-6 portions and place on the plates. Pipe on the mash, add the glazed carrots and roasted onions, then finish with the sauce.

PASTA ON THE ITALIAN ROUTE

Founded by Gian & Pasquale, North Town brings contemporary Italian-style cookery to the heart of Sheffield.

These close friends and partners in crime have bridged the gap between the cobbled streets of Naples and the seven hills of Sheffield with classic Italian dishes, divine drink offerings and, of course, their cheeky sense of humour as they invite you to join them on a journey back to Campania and beyond.

Located on Abbeydale Road, North Town began spontaneously. Reacting to global pandemic restrictions, the duo realised the opportunity to provide locals with a takeaway favourite: coffee and cannolis! As news spread fast about this new spot providing tasty treats, the offerings expanded to a mouthwatering meatball phenomenon: a highly sought-after panino constructed with Sicilian meatballs, San Marzano tomatoes, melted taleggio, homemade ciabatta and a whole lotta love.

It was the perfect entry point and allowed the business to gain real momentum. As destiny worked in their favour, the unit next door became available and what began as a weekend pop-up shop flourished into a unique dining experience built on passion, knowledge and the desire to feed one's senses.

The name has no real back story – only that it was an against-the-clock decision with a sprinkling of added pressure to come up with a URL. Nothing romantic, unfortunately, for all those Italian love-story seekers. However, the walls of 699-701 Abbeydale Rd are plastered with history and Gian's personal collection of '1942 La Gazzetta Dello Sport'. They've given the former bakery and guitar shop a new lease of life, transforming it into a palazzo of eccentricity, adorned with sporting memorabilia and its own venerable quirks.

North Town pride themselves on offering high-quality produce at a very honest price. There's a distinct Southern Italian slant on their dishes – from Pesce Spada to Orechiette, you will be spoilt for choice. While you're ordering, an in-house sommelier will be on-hand to recommend the perfect wine, or if you fancy exploring their impressive vermouth collection, their negronis are the best in town!

Trust is the main ingredient here. Insider knowledge and recommendations are often dished out (free of charge), which has naturally led to the next extension of the business: an imminent food and travel channel by the name of foodpilgrims.com. This exciting venture will eliminate all of those wasted hours of swiping through endless TripAdvisor reviews and provide the honest expertise you need to plan your travels.

Drawn in by the initial intrigue of this quirky little eatery, you will leave with the desire to return again and again. So, take a step through the door that never disappears and digest the authenticity, the flavour and the flair. You won't regret it.

Leave the gun
Take the Cannoli

BITTER
CAMPARI

EST. 2020
NORTH TOWN
ITALIAN STORE & DINING ROOM POP-UP
TAKEAWAY
ORDER HERE

NORTH TOWN'S SICILIAN MEATBALLS

Preparation time: 10 minutes | Cooking time: 10 minutes | Serves 5

This is the recipe for our famous North Town lamb meatballs! We have made thousands and thousands of portions of these over the few years we have been open. Whether they are baked in our NT sugo with melted taleggio or served on our crunchy ciabatta, they are always a winner!

55g raisins
1kg lamb mince
25g ground almonds
10g salt
5g ground black pepper
Chilli flakes, to taste
1 preserved lemon
2 sprigs of fresh mint
Olive oil, to shallow fry

Start by soaking the raisins in hot water and set aside. Place the lamb mince in a bowl with the ground almonds, salt, pepper and chilli flakes.

Drain the raisins, chop them roughly and add to the bowl. Finely chop the preserved lemon and add to the bowl. Pick the mint leaves, chop them up and add to the rest of the ingredients.

Mix the contents of the bowl thoroughly with your hands so everything is combined evenly. Roll the mixture into 45g balls.

Heat up a frying pan on a medium to high heat and add a good glug of olive oil. Place the meatballs in the frying pan, leaving a small space between them. Wait 4-5 minutes for them to colour nicely before using a pair of tongs to turn them all over. Cook on the other side until nicely coloured again, then stir and shake the pan to colour the edges (be careful as the meatballs will have released a fair bit of hot fat).

Once coloured, give the meatballs a squeeze and if they are nice and springy, they will be ready. We serve them in our tomato sugo, baked in the oven with taleggio cheese, or why not put them in a crusty ciabatta with a bit of sugo and cheese!

THE ALPHA AND...

Omega at Abbeydale is a restaurant, bar and function room in the pavilion of a sports club, offering an ideal venue for corporate and private events in the south of Sheffield.

Co-owners Jamie and Steve took over in 2018, bringing with them many years of experience from their previous home at Baldwins Omega. A brand new restaurant was built at the Abbeydale Sports Club prior to the changeover, accompanied by a full renovation and redecoration of the existing bar and function room. Although the venue is popular with the sporting crowd, you don't have to be a member to enjoy everything Omega at Abbeydale has to offer.

The relaxed restaurant serves traditional food with a twist, offering set two or three course menus that are updated monthly alongside a specials board. Maple glazed salmon, roast rump of lamb, blue cheese and leek tart or pan-fried calves' liver are just some examples of the delicious dishes you might find there. Local suppliers include William Howe for the fish and Doug Hebdige for meats, ensuring top quality produce all year round. Jamie and Steve have always been committed to oven to table food that's cooked and served fresh, whether they are catering for the many or the few.

The function room at Omega can host up to 120 people and provides the ideal venue for party nights or banquets which have specially created menus for larger events. From live music to seasonal dining experiences (not to mention the unmissable office Christmas parties complete with a themed nightclub!) they are experts in creating a great atmosphere and, of course, great food and drink. The wine list in the restaurant and the hand-pulled bitters on the bar, alongside a selection of lagers and gins, ensures that everyone can find their favourite tipple.

Already a popular spot with lots of regular customers, Omega at Abbeydale also scooped the title of Best Newcomer in the 2019 Westside Restaurant Awards. Jamie and Steve are looking forward to building the business up after the difficulties of the last few years, especially for the parties and functions that they were renowned for at Baldwins. "Hospitality is in our bones," says Jamie, "and it's still a joy to be working with new people and familiar faces here at Omega every day."

ABBEYDALE
SPORTS CLUB
omega
AT ABBEYDALE
estaurant Banqueting Bar Terrace
ABBEYDALE
SQUASH

ASSIETTE OF FISH WITH SULTANA RICE AND LENTIL DAHL

Preparation time: 20 minutes | Cooking time: 1 hour 10 minutes | Serves 4 as a starter

This dish was created for an Indian themed dinner which was held annually at Baldwins Omega.

800ml vegetable stock
1 tin of coconut milk
100g lentils
1 onion, finely chopped
3 cloves of garlic, minced
3 tsp madras curry powder
80g basmati rice
30g sultanas
2 sprigs of coriander, chopped
200g portions of monkfish, cod, and seabass
4 tiger prawns
½ a fresh mango, diced
1 tsp onion seeds

Combine the stock, coconut milk, lentils, onion, garlic and curry powder in a saucepan. Simmer for 1 hour until the lentils are soft and you have a nice thick dahl.

Meanwhile, cook the rice and then refresh it under cold running water. Drain the rice thoroughly, then fry it with the sultanas and chopped coriander.

Cut each piece of fish into 4 equal portions and fry them along with the tiger prawns in a clean pan for 2 minutes on either side. Let the fish and prawns rest while you lightly fry the mango.

Plate the fish and prawns with the sultana rice, lentil dahl and mango. Sprinkle with the onion seeds to finish.

BRAISED PIG'S CHEEKS WITH KIDNEY, APPLE PURÉE & MASH

Preparation time: 25 minutes | Cooking time: 2 hours 20 minutes | Serves 2

This inexpensive dish is full of flavour, using a long slow cook and often overlooked cuts of meat to create a budget-friendly dinner that will still impress your family and friends.

4 inner pig cheek muscles
1 onion, finely chopped
2 cloves of garlic
5 sage leaves
2 apples
400g Maris Piper potatoes
Knob of butter
1 pig's kidney, diced and de-piped

Pan fry the pig's cheeks to seal them and then place in an ovenproof dish with half the chopped onion, the garlic cloves and a couple of sage leaves. Add 500ml of warm water and place in the oven for 2 hours at 140°c until tender.

Pour the juices from the cheeks into a saucepan and reduce by half, then season to taste. Meanwhile, peel and chop the apples. Place them in a bowl with a splash of water and microwave until soft, then blend to a purée.

Peel and chop the potatoes, then boil until tender. Drain and mash with the butter. Lastly, pan fry the diced kidney in a hot pan for a couple of minutes.

Keep everything warm until you are ready to plate up, then garnish with the remaining sage leaves.

A TASTE OF SOUTH AFRICA

The Orange Bird is one of few places in the UK where you can find modern South African food cooked on a braai by a professional chef, and Sheffielders are lucky enough to have this neighbourhood restaurant right in the heart of Hillsborough.

Having opened in November 2020 during one of many Covid lockdowns, The Orange Bird has had to adapt and evolve its offering since the very beginning. This process of development included shifting from takeaway food to casual dining and creating a unique style along the way. Chef Matt grew up in South Africa and moved to the UK when he was 15, where he embarked on a career in kitchens that replaced the braai of his childhood with Michelin-starred cooking. He always enjoyed working with barbecues, though, and when they decided to hold a South African food night at The Orange Bird in its first year, something just clicked.

Matt's modern approach to South African cuisine, along with the inspiration he took from other international food and great chefs he'd worked with or admired, went down a storm with customers. He and Anne, who are business partners and co-owners of the restaurant, decided that this was the right direction for The Orange Bird to move in. The menu is still evolving all the time, as Matt and sous chef Sophie work on perfecting staple dishes – such as the peri peri chicken that everybody loves – as well as exploring new ideas. They are careful to avoid creating a pastiche of South African food, however, which itself is so varied and features many different cultures. It also tends to be heavy on the meat, whereas The Orange Bird aims to cater for vegetarians just as much as carnivores!

The Orange Bird is not just about the food though, as the carefully curated drinks menu features handcrafted cocktails alongside all the South African wines, beers, whiskies and mezcal that Anne and Matt can source. Word has already spread to ex-pat South Africans, Afrikaans and Zimbabwean emigrants who travel from all over the UK to visit The Orange Bird and enjoy nostalgic treats like the Peppermint Crisp tart, made from a much-loved South African chocolate bar. They also have lots of local regulars, and as residents of the area themselves, Anne and Matt are proud to have brought such a popular addition to Hillsborough's high street.

The restaurant is small, intimate and casual which allows people to feel comfortable whether they want dinner out or just a few drinks. The Orange Bird is purposefully not the kind of place or price point reserved for special occasions, but a friendly neighbourhood hangout with both South Africa and Sheffield in its heart.

the
Orange
Bird
Neighbourhood
Kitchen
S6

CARAMELISED AUBERGINE WITH HONEY LABNEH

Preparation time: 40 minutes, plus 8-24 hours for the labneh | Cooking time: 10 minutes | Serves 4

This recipe is inspired by a beautiful aubergine dish from Pachamama London. Matt also created the dish to highlight some of the lesser known South African cuisines, in this case the Malay cuisine from the Cape area.

For the honey labneh

200g natural yoghurt
5g Maldon salt & 50g honey

For the chilli seaweed sambal

15 dried chillies
15g dried kombu sheet
15g lightly toasted nori
6 Thai shallots
3 cloves of garlic, peeled
2 tbsp light soft brown sugar
1 tbsp gochujang
2 tsp red miso
½ tsp fine sea salt
1 tbsp vegetable oil

For the cucumber sambal

½ cucumber & ½ onion
1 clove of garlic
1 inch fresh ginger & ½ red chilli
1 tbsp each chopped coriander and chopped mint
½ lime, juiced
1 tsp sugar & splash of tamari

For the caramelised aubergine

2 aubergines & 1 onion
100g potato flour
Handful of fresh mint

For the honey labneh

This part is best completed the day before, or on the morning of the day you're eating the dish. Combine the yoghurt and salt, then hang in a linen or muslin cloth to drain for 8 to 24 hours. When it's finished straining, mix in the honey.

For the chilli seaweed sambal

Soak the chillies and kombu, separately, in hot water to rehydrate. Halve and deseed the chillies. Lightly toast the nori to bring back the freshness and fragrance by laying the nori sheets over a toaster or in a hot pan. Combine all the ingredients, apart from the oil, in a food processor and whizz until smooth. Heat the oil in a pan, add the sambal and cook until fragrant, then set aside until later.

For the cucumber sambal

Peel the cucumber, halve it lengthways, then scoop out the seeds and discard. Halve again lengthways and then chop into 1cm pieces. Dice the onion as small as you can, mince the garlic, and finely grate the ginger. Deseed the red chilli and chop finely. Add all the ingredients except the cucumber to a medium size bowl and mix well, then add the cucumber and mix again.

For the caramelised aubergine

Heat some vegetable oil in a deep fat fryer or large pan. Peel the aubergine and cut into quarters lengthways, then cut each quarter into 6 large chunks. Thinly slice the onion.

Coat the aubergine chunks in the potato flour and fry at 150°c for roughly 5 minutes, until lightly coloured. Do this in batches so as not to overcrowd the pan. Coat the onions in the potato flour, add them to the oil with the aubergine and continue to cook for another minute, then drain on kitchen paper. Coat everything in a tablespoon of the chilli sambal.

To assemble

Put a generous amount of the honey labneh in the centre of your plate or bowl, followed by 12 pieces of the aubergine and some of the crispy onions. Finally, add the cucumber sambal and garnish with fresh mint.

CATERING FOR ALL SEASONS

For bespoke menus designed to tick all the boxes at any event, PJ taste have the experience and knowledge to serve up a feast of homegrown, locally sourced and foraged food and drink.

PJ taste have been serving seasonally inspired local food for large corporate dinners, weddings and events in Sheffield since 2006. The caterers travel to venues all over Sheffield, South Yorkshire and North East Derbyshire as well as welcoming people to their own charming meeting, dining and event space in Attercliffe. They offer a wide range of food to suit many occasions, such as large-scale fine dining dinners, lunches with a street food theme (think barbecues and wood-fired pizza), innovative breakfast canapes, business buffet lunches, handmade cakes and quality locally roasted coffee.

Owners Peter and John have put their strong values at the heart of PJ taste since the beginning, including sustainability and local sourcing. They have operated an electric delivery vehicle since 2015, which is recharged by the 37 solar panels on their venue's roof in Attercliffe! The kitchen is zero waste, which ensures every element of an ingredient is utilised, from breadcrumbs made from excess crusts to stocks and gravies from bones. Any final organic waste is used for compost in their permaculture style of growing which encompasses fruit trees, interesting perennial vegetables and a large number of honeybee colonies.

"We are proud to grow all our own edible flowers, much soft fruit and apples, plums and pears in the forest garden on our plot. Our bees are treatment free and provide amazing honey for our Sheffield hampers and for cakes and baking in the kitchen. Alongside our own harvest, we use an array of excellent local food producers."

PJ taste recently catered for the Sheffield Business Awards with a bespoke menu including their ever popular Sheffield Egg, Wateralls Pork Pie, Casa Gomez Chorizo, Hedgerow Preserves chutney, a Moss Valley Meats pork fillet and cider from Woodthrope Hall to name just a few of their favourite local producers. Other regular clients include The University of Sheffield, the Sheffield Chamber, Sheffield Museums Trust, Asseal, Wake Smith, Twinkle and St Lukes. As a family business, PJ taste works with a multi-skilled one team approach. They are keen to continuously learn and improve through creative processes and are also striving to develop the next generation of chefs and caterers by working with Sheffield College through the PJ taste academy to secure a great future.

FILO FETA PARCELS WITH LOCAL HONEY AND BEETROOT SALAD

Preparation time: 50 minutes | Cooking time: 1 hour 15 minutes | Serves 6

A lovely summery dish invoking lazy days on a Greek island but made with some Sheffield touches.

For the filo feta parcels

200g block of feta cheese

30ml olive oil

Small bunch of fresh herbs, finely chopped (we used rosemary and marjoram from our plot, but you can use dried if fresh herbs aren't available)

Sea salt and black pepper

2 tbsp local runny honey

250g packet of filo pastry

For the beetroot salad

1 lemon, juiced

1 orange, juiced

2 tsp Dijon mustard

250ml light olive oil

600g fresh beetroot

1 red onion

Bunch of fresh parsley

It's great to use a local raw honey which preserves all the natural enzymes and pollen that the bees produce. The July crop from our bees has a wonderful depth of flavour with the initial sweetness tempered by the slightly spicy tastes of blackberry and rose bay willow herb flowers. We like to use the amazing organic salads and vegetables from growers like Regather based in Sheffield's Moss Valley. Their beetroot has a wonderful earthy flavour which you just know is good for your health as well as your soul!

For the filo feta parcels

Cut your feta block into 0.5-1cm slices and then into triangles roughly 6cm along each side. Place these on a plate with a little olive oil and scatter with the chopped herbs, season with salt and pepper, then drizzle with the honey.

Next, cut the filo sheets into rectangles a little wider than the feta triangles. Take a sheet and brush with olive oil, then place a second and third sheet on top to create layers, brushing each sheet with oil as you go. Place a feta triangle at one end and fold it over on itself twice within the pastry, keeping the triangle shape. Leave the edge underneath and press slightly so the oil seals the parcel. These can be made an hour or so ahead and refrigerated until cooking, or even frozen at this stage.

When ready to cook the parcels, place them into a hot oven at 190°c for 15 minutes. They are done when they have become really crisp and started to take on a golden colour.

For the beetroot salad

First, make the dressing. The easiest and quickest way is to add the citrus juices, Dijon mustard and olive oil to a lidded jar with salt and pepper to taste, then give it a vigorous shake to emulsify.

Next, the fresh beetroot needs cooking. Either place the whole root in oiled foil and bake in the oven or simmer in a pan just covered with water, having cleaned off any soil first. When cooked, they can be cooled in cold water and then the skin can be easily peeled with a knife.

Cut the cooked beetroot into 1cm cubes, slice the red onion into thin rings and finely chop the parsley. To assemble the salad, toss the beetroot, onion and parsley together with some of the vinaigrette dressing and extra salt and pepper. Taste to check you have added enough seasoning and dressing, remembering that the feta parcels are already quite salty.

To serve, arrange the beetroot salad on a plate or bowl and place the warm filo triangles on top.

RACK OF LAMB WITH LOCAL REDCURRANT JELLY

Preparation time: 35 minutes | Cooking time: 20 minutes | Serves 4

Rack of lamb is definitely a dish for a special occasion; it makes an impressive main course but is one of the more expensive cuts.

8 rib French trimmed rack of lamb (or 2 racks for those with bigger appetites; see above)
Sea salt and black pepper
25ml olive oil

For the redcurrant jus
200ml red wine
50g redcurrant jelly
1 tsp balsamic vinegar
500ml chicken stock
25g butter

Traditionally, people allow 3-4 ribs per person but in the spirit of reducing our overall meat consumption we have found that 2-3 ribs per person is sufficient as long as you are buying quality local meat which has been well butchered. We use Andrews butchers in Rotherham who source lamb from Wortley. We make lovely redcurrant jelly each July from the crop of berries harvested on our plot and highly recommend this type of perennial growing (the bushes require very little work!) or choosing a good local brand.

The redcurrant jus can be made a day ahead (or made in a bigger batch and frozen) if time is of the essence. Reduce the red wine, redcurrant jelly and balsamic vinegar by up to 25% of the original volume in a pan until the mixture is starting to get sticky. Add the chicken stock and reduce again by about half. At this stage, cool and store the jus if using later, or keep it warm ready for finishing when the lamb is cooked.

For the lamb, preheat your oven to 180°c and heat a large ovenproof frying pan over a high heat. Season the lamb all over with salt and pepper and coat with the olive oil, then sear in the hot frying pan until it is nicely coloured all over. Transfer the pan to the oven or place the lamb onto a lined baking tray if your pan is not ovenproof. Cook the lamb rack for 15 minutes and then remove from the oven, cover with foil and allow to rest for 5 minutes before carving.

While the lamb is resting, finish the redcurrant jus. Bring it to a simmer and whisk in the butter to give the jus a rich glossy finish.

To serve

Carve the rib joint into single cutlets and serve 2-3 ribs per person along with your chosen potatoes and vegetables. Add a little redcurrant jus to each plate or serve it separately in a gravy jug.

BLACKCURRANT SORBET WITH HAZELNUT CRUNCH

Preparation time: 120 minutes, plus churning/freezing time | Cooking time: 10 minutes | Serves 6

Blackcurrants are an easy to grow perennial fruit which give a great crop every June and July on our plot. They are a little safer than the redcurrants as the birds seem to avoid stealing blackcurrants but definitely target redcurrants!

For the hazelnut crunch

4 tbsp light olive oil (or pomace oil)
20g rosemary leaves
1 lemon, zested and juiced
200g hazelnuts
2 tbsp local runny honey

For the sorbet

200ml boiling water
200g sugar
4 tbsp liquid glucose
750g blackcurrants
2 lemons, juiced

Blackberries are quite tart on their own but this delicious sorbet creates a refreshing dessert which highlights the fruit's flavour. We use our spring honey for the hazelnut crunch, and you could complete the local sourcing by foraging for hazelnuts in the Autumn.

For the hazelnut crunch

The hazelnut crunch can be made ahead and stored in an airtight container for up to 3 days. Heat the oil in a frying pan on a medium heat, then add the rosemary and lemon zest to bring out the natural oils, moving them around for 30 seconds or so.

Add the hazelnuts and stir for a minute or two until they take on some colour. Finally, add the honey and lemon juice. Allow the mixture to caramelise just for another 30 seconds or so. Cool and then smash into shards ready for your sorbet garnish.

For the sorbet

Add the boiling water to the sugar in a pan big enough to hold the rest of the ingredients. When the sugar has dissolved, add the glucose syrup and the blackberries to the pan and cook until the fruit is soft (approximately 5 minutes). Using a food processor or stick blender, whizz up the mixture until smooth and then stir in the lemon juice.

At this stage, for a super smooth sorbet you can pass the mixture through a sieve. Otherwise, leave as it is for a sorbet with more texture.

Transfer the mixture to an ice cream maker and churn until set into a scoopable texture. Alternatively, place the sorbet in your freezer and remove it 3 or 4 times to beat the mixture with a fork while it freezes. Store the sorbet in the freezer for up to 3 months, removing it 5-10 minutes before serving to soften. Serve with shards of the hazelnut crunch and possibly edible flowers.

TASTES DIVINE

Without a doubt the grandest entrance to any coffee shop in the city, 1554 Café offers some heavenly respite for Sheffield foodies.

Sheffield Cathedral has been an iconic landmark in the heart of the city for centuries, with some parts of the building's structure dating back to c. 1200. Today it continues to play a vital role as a cornerstone of the local community, and neatly squirrelled away inside this historic building you'll find 1554 Coffee & Gift Shop, a peaceful retreat showcasing quality produce from local suppliers.

With ample comfy seating and a welcoming attitude to all, 1554 serves all day throughout the week and has won a number of accolades including the coveted Sheffield City Centre Retail Award for outstanding service. They only use local suppliers for the food and drinks, so you'll be able to enjoy the likes of Bakewell Bakery, Secret Cake Club, Our Cow Molly and their own specially designed house blend from Heavenly Coffee amongst many others.

Food-wise, they're famed for their brownies, meat pies and Mrs Wilson's sticky fruit cake. Initially opening in June 2015, they have since built up a strong reputation as a tranquil oasis tucked away from the hustle and bustle of town; a venue which strives to give back to the wider community through sharing their friendly space with all and using it to promote the work of local artisans and makers. The message of community and charity is reflected in the name itself, inspired by a Royal Charter which returned property and land to the people of Sheffield on 8th June 1554.

Alongside the 1554 Café, the cathedral also houses a popular gift shop. Now under the watchful eye of manager Ruth, the café and shop go in hand in hand; much of the local produce they use in the café can be purchased in the shop, and vice versa. This includes the Sheffield honey providing a sweet kick on some of the desserts, special bottles of Henderson's Relish splashed over their famous pies, and even the prints from local photographers providing décor can be purchased as postcards.

When you're finished perusing, you're welcome to explore centuries of history detailed across the building, ogle at the impressive lantern tower designed by Amber Hiscot or simply take a minute to embrace the peaceful atmosphere emanating from this inspirational space. Pop by the next time you're in town for a morning pick-me-up or mouth-watering lunch!

ZINGY LEMON DRIZZLE LOAF

Preparation time: 15 minutes | Cooking time: 30-40 minutes | Makes 3 x 1lb loaf cakes (each loaf generously serves 4-6)

This cake is a firm favourite with everyone, full of zesty lemony goodness. Top tip: whizz the sugar and lemon zest together first, to release more lemon oil from the zest for extra zing!

120g butter or good quality margarine
300g caster sugar
2 tbsp baking powder
2 large lemons, zested
360ml milk
3 large eggs

For the drizzle

100g granulated sugar
1-2 lemons, juiced

Preheat your oven to 150°c fan and line 3 x 1lb loaf tins with a suitable liner, or grease and line with baking parchment. Alternatively, you can purchase 'bake in' rigid card disposable loaf cases.

Rub the butter or margarine into all the dry ingredients and lemon zest (you can do this in a stand mixer if you have one).

Mix the wet ingredients together and whisk lightly with a fork, then add half the wet mixture into the dry ingredients and mix well. Add the remaining milk and egg mixture while whisking carefully until just combined.

Divide the cake mixture between the tins (roughly 450g each) and bake for 30 minutes in the preheated oven. Turn the tins round so the cakes bake evenly, then leave them in the oven for a further 10-15 minutes until springy and golden on top.

For the drizzle, combine the granulated sugar with the lemon juice until well combined. Spoon it over the cakes while they are still cooling in the tins.

Serve the lemon drizzle cakes warm with vanilla ice cream, or cold by the slice. They will keep for 3-4 days in the fridge but are best eaten at room temperature.

ALL FIRED UP

For hot sauces that won't all have you breathing fire but are packed with flavour and fun, Sheffield Dragon has made a big name for itself in a very short time.

The spark for Sheffield Dragon was lit in 2019, when Andrew Armstrong made a chilli pickle for the family's Christmas cheeseboard. Having made enough to give away as stocking fillers, friends and family kept asking him for more. When the pandemic hit in 2020, Andrew worked reduced hours for most of the year and decided to establish a business to make and sell tasty homemade chilli products in his spare time. His wife's colleague suggested the name, which they both loved straight away, and Andrew designed the logo himself to make the jars and bottles really stand out in the crowd. When a few local shops decided to stock the range, he knew he was onto something.

Sheffield Dragon's range has been developed with all levels of flavour and heat in mind. "I like to think there is something for most palates, as we go from not-so-hot to very hot, but what I think really stands out is that even the hottest flavours we have are so well balanced you're not overwhelmed with heat," says Andrew. All his products are also designed to be versatile for use in everyday cooking, whether that's a pickle, barbecue rub or hot sauce. One restaurant even uses the hottest sauce to make a vegan nduja and Andrew's other catering customers are always using the products in interesting and innovative ways.

As a child, Andrew hated not being able to enjoy the things others ate due to food allergies, so he also pays particular attention to making Sheffield Dragon products vegan friendly and additive-free without added allergens, with plans to develop more sauces especially for people who are allergic to the allium family, which includes onions and garlic. Andrew attributes the company's success partly to this ethos of listening to and learning from customers, creating an inclusive and aspirational business environment which has allowed him to expand from the home kitchen to an artisan preserves facility in less than two years.

Sheffield Dragon often collaborates with other companies too and creates customised products for specific occasions, most recently the bestselling Renegade Mango hot sauce which was developed in collaboration with Renegade Brass Band. They are stocked in lots of shops around the Steel City, as well as being used in more and more restaurants and catering services. Andrew hopes to open a brand-new production facility in 2023, looking to continue his expansion within the world of tasty homemade chilli products throughout Sheffield and beyond.

ROASTED JALAPENO
SCORPION BBQ SAUCE
THE SCORPION'S TALE
HOT FUZZZ
SCOTCH MIX
LEMON DROP HOP
KIWI SUPER GREEN
BOTTLE THIS FIRE

HEFFIELD
DRAGON

Renegade Mango
GIN

Renegade Mango

MAKERS
·STORE·

THE DRAGONI

Preparation time: 5 minutes | Serves 1

This came about as I really fancied trying an alternative to a Bloody Mary using one of my sauces, Renegade Mango, which pairs mango and yellow habanero for a fantastic medium heat and unctuous texture. I spent a few weeks perfecting the cocktail recipe and have been so pleased to see it being served in some bars in Sheffield already!

250ml orange juice
50ml good London style gin
15ml Renegade Mango
Handful of ice
Dash of Campari

Measure out the orange juice, gin and Renegade Mango into a cocktail shaker over plenty of ice. Shake briskly for a minute or two.

Serve The Dragoni in a cocktail glass, either strained or straight from the shaker (but leave the ice in the shaker). Stir in a dash of Campari and enjoy!

HEFFIELD
DRAGON Chilli Sauce
Renegade Mango

IT'S THE BEE'S KNEES

Jez Daughtry has been producing honey for over 12 years in Sheffield and Derbyshire, resulting in a unique product that celebrates its origins and the many other small businesses who support it.

The Sheffield Honey Company was launched in 2010 at the very first Sheffield Food Festival, after a year of preparation by Jez and his wife Alison. Following a background in IT and a redundancy, Jez decided to embark on an idea he'd already been exploring: producing honey in the city of Sheffield. He knew there was a gap in the market for a small local brand, with great design and a clear ethos, to make waves with a delicious natural product. What Jez hadn't bargained on was just how much hard work would go into the building of a business that could become financially sustainable in the face of many weather-dependant and physically demanding challenges that came with beekeeping.

Thanks to the support of his family and a steep learning curve, The Sheffield Honey Company has become an integral part of the city's foodie landscape, from jars on the shelves of numerous local retailers to hives on the roof of Weston Park Museum. DED Studio have always done the branding for the labels, which proudly flies the flag for Sheffield in name and nature. Jez's relationships with these fellow independents are one of his proudest achievements, who include top restaurants JÖRO and Rafters as well as stockists from Chatsworth House to the smallest grocer's.

The honey itself is dictated by the seasons and what the bees are pollinating at different times of the year. Spring and summer blossom honeys are flavoured with flowering trees and plants including sycamore, hawthorn and dandelions and then lime trees, brambles and privets to name just a few. Jez also produces a soft set blossom honey which naturally crystallises, then borage honey from July which has a light, mild and nutty flavour before the intensely aromatic heather honey in August and September. In October, the honey is harvested and the bees are tucked up for winter, ready to do it all again next year. Jez currently has around 280 colonies of bees across Derbyshire and Sheffield, using an eclectic mix of apiary sites and paying the landowners in honey as is tradition.

"We've had a fantastic year despite the heat waves and floods," says Jez, "partly because I've been doing this long enough to have made a lot of mistakes and learnt how to manage these things. Alison and I still ask ourselves how on earth we got here but it's been great; I think we've done something very special in Sheffield and long may it all continue."

IN SHEFFIELD
BLOSSOM HONEY
340 g/12 oz
THE
SHEFFIELD HONEY
COMPANY
PRODUCE OF ENGLAND
WWW.SHEFFIELD-HONEY.CO.UK
BEST BEFORE DATE
End2022

ROASTED PEAKLAND WHITE, CURRIED GRANOLA & SHEFFIELD HONEY

Preparation time: 15 minutes | Cooking time: 30 minutes | Serves 2 as a snack (1 as light dinner)

Peakland White is a feta-style cheese made in the Peak District, which is the perfect partner for a curried twist on Elm's house granola and the delicate flavours of locally produced blossom honey. This recipe was created by Elm for the Sheffield Honey Company.

For the granola

50g unsalted butter
50g Sheffield Honey
½ tsp ground cinnamon
100g rolled oats
125g mixed nuts
25g coconut quills
35g sunflower seeds
35g pumpkin seeds
10g sesame seeds
10g flax seeds
1 tsp curry powder
Pinch of flaky salt

For the cheese

125g Peakland White
Drizzle of olive or rapeseed oil
2 tbsp Sheffield Blossom Honey
1 lime, halved
Flatbreads, to serve

For the granola

Preheat the oven to 170°c. Melt the butter, honey and cinnamon together in a pan on a gentle heat. Combine all the dry ingredients, except the curry powder and salt in a large bowl. Pour the melted butter mixture into the bowl and mix until the dry ingredients are coated.

Spread the granola mix out on a baking tray and bake for 10 minutes. Stir and then bake for 5 more minutes. Remove from the oven and leave to cool, then break it up. Weigh out 20g of the granola and combine this with the curry powder and salt. Store the remaining granola in an airtight container to enjoy at breakfast.

For the cheese

Turn up the oven temperature to 180°c and oil the base of an ovenproof tray or plate. Place the Peakland White on the oiled tray or plate and drizzle a little more oil on top.

Gently spread the curried granola on top of the cheese, drizzle with a little more oil and then bake for 10 minutes.

Meanwhile, heat the honey with the juice of half the lime in a pan. Let this reduce a little to create a syrup. Once the cheese is ready, pour some of the honey and lime syrup over the top and decant the rest into a small vessel for adding as you go. Zest the remaining lime half over the cheese and serve. Enjoy with warm flatbreads while the cheese is still hot and gooey.

I'M HOOKED!

This longstanding family business prides itself on sourcing the best quality produce as directly as possible to offer a huge array of fish and seafood species. From Strawberry Grouper to Blue Swimming Crab, you name it, they've got it!

Smith & Tissington is a family business in The Moor Market, focusing mainly on fresh fish, fresh shellfish, seafood, frozen produce and eggs. It was established by Roy and Mary Tissington over 70 years ago, and was passed down to their son Paul Tissington, whose wife Debra also played an important role in the business. It's now run by Paul's son, Mathew Tissington.

Over the years they have built an outstanding supply base, meaning that most fresh produce they sell is bought directly from Shetland Auction and Brixham Auction as well as multiple different salmon farms, in addition to imported supply from India, Sri Lanka and Senegal. All of this can be tracked back to the exact boat that landed the fish. Availability can change every week due to seasonality, and weather can also play a big factor in the amount of produce available on each auction market.

Something that Smith & Tissington are looking to build on in the future is their knowledge of cooking, to enable them to offer better advice on cooking the different kinds of fish and seafood they sell. "In my opinion, out of all the different types of fish we sell, my favourite would have to be either kingfish, scallops, turbot or of course salmon, although a new favourite with our customers in the past few weeks has been cobia," says Mathew.

As with any market stall or small family business, the business is built on the regular support and loyalty of the customers who shop week in, week out. This is thanks to the team's drive to provide excellent service and the best produce at a fair price. Mathew's day starts around 3-4am when he'll analyse the market landings and decide what he should be looking to buy for that day's upcoming auctions. Once the fish has been purchased at the Brixham Auction that morning, the market stall receives its produce around 20 hours later, very early the following morning. All imports are shipped directly to ensure maximum freshness, usually taking a maximum of 36-40 hours from leaving Senegal, Sri Lanka or India to their arrival at Smith & Tissington.

"The Moor Market as a whole is the best in terms of quality, range of products and prices that you can find in Sheffield," says Mathew. "It offers a huge range of products from independent, local businesses for whom every sale is important, and we're proud to be part of it."

Smith & Tissington
Fresh Fish & Poultry Since 1960
Farm Fresh Eggs
Fresh Tuna Steak
£19.98 Per Kilo

SALMON FILLET, LEMON & THYME CRUMB, BASIL PESTO

Preparation time: 25 minutes | Cooking time: 40 minutes | Serves 4

Salmon makes a perfect quick and easy meal; you can bake, pan fry, grill, or poach and it's also healthy, high in protein and omega-3 fatty acids. The crunchy herb and citrus crumb and the rich basil pesto both balance out perfectly with the earthiness of the new potatoes and greens.

500g new potatoes
200g white bread or sourdough, cut into small chunks
4 thyme sprigs, picked
1 lemon, zested
30g olive oil
4 x 180g salmon fillets
3 cloves of garlic, crushed
30g butter
Small bunch of parsley, chopped
400g seasonal greens

For the homemade pesto
20g pine nuts
50g basil
30g parmesan
1 small clove of garlic
Pinch of salt
Pinch of pepper
120ml olive oil

For the homemade pesto

To make the pesto, toast the pine nuts and cool, and then add all the dry ingredients into a food processor and blitz. While blitzing, slowly add in the olive oil and keep blending until smooth. Keep the pesto in an airtight container and refrigerate until needed. You can also use a good quality shop-bought pesto for this recipe.

Preheat the oven to 200°c.

Place the new potatoes in a saucepan, cover with water and season with salt. Bring to the boil and simmer for approximately 15-20 minutes until tender, and then strain.

Place the bread chunks, thyme, lemon zest and olive oil into a food processor and blitz until you have a fine breadcrumb.

Take an oven tray and line with baking paper; place the salmon fillets on the tray, drizzle with a little oil and season with a pinch of salt, then cook in the oven for 10 minutes. Remove the salmon and evenly sprinkle with the herb crumb, and then place back in the oven for 6-8 minutes, until the crumb is golden brown. While the salmon is cooking, steam your choice of greens for the required time according to personal preference.

Just before you are ready to serve, use the pan the potatoes were cooked in, add the crushed garlic and butter and gently cook on a medium-low heat for a few minutes. Next, add the potatoes and parsley, and then gently crush with a fork and season with salt and pepper.

Serve with the steamed seasonal greens, new potatoes and a drizzle of pesto.

WAKE ME UP BEFORE YOU COCOA

Sorrel's Cocoa Bakery is a Sheffield-based, handmade chocolate and bakes maker, with 'little pink shops' in Crookes and Bakewell.

A self-confessed chocaholic, Sorrel Botham began working with chocolate in 2014, initially as a hobby and way to do something that made her happy. It wasn't until she started receiving rave reviews for her creations that she began heading out to farmers' markets and independent shops to hawk her sweet treats. During this time, there were no immediate plans for a shop, and it wasn't until she spotted a rundown shopfront, with unwelcoming steel bars across the windows, that she thought, 'perfect, that's the place for me!'

She then set about lovingly restoring the Crookes site, giving it a sweet makeover and taking inspiration from the colour schemes she had used to sketch out her dream shop in notebooks years before. In 2018 she opened the shop with just one helper, making all the bakes and treats from home, in her master bedroom!

Fast-forward to today, and she now employs eight people, has recently opened a second shop in Bakewell, and has her own kitchen and office space in Attercliffe, serving both sites. What often surprises many visitors is that all the chocolatey products available in the shop are made in-house. The sheer variety of sugary goodness also set Sorrel's apart. From exquisite chocolate bonbons and truffles that you might find in a high-end chocolatier, to hearty brownies and cakes you would expect in your favourite café, there's truly something for everyone.

Coffee and hot drinks are also available at the Crookes site, which of course include indulgent hot chocolates with melting caramel Freddo stirrers, while out in Bakewell soft serve ice cream, with flavours that incorporate the bakes, are becoming a real crowd pleaser.

The bakes are made fresh each day, with the flavours changed up on a weekly basis, whereas the bonbons come in a core range, with new flavours added whenever something new takes Sorrel's fancy. New products are hitting the shelves all the time, some of which are suggestions from their loyal army of sweet-toothed customers.

Sorrel estimates around 75% of weekly custom is from returning customers and she is thankful to the 'lovely' local community in and around Crookes for their support over the previous four years, particularly during the difficult period of national lockdown.

While a lockdown was challenging, it also gave Sorrel the opportunity to expand her online offering, which has since gone from strength to strength, dispatching orders across the country.

"It's been a real whirlwind," says Sorrel, "especially over lockdown, but I love doing it and I'll always love it. The dream would be to open a couple of more shops in Sheffield to share our treats with more of our favourite city and collaborate with more amazing local independents."

Brownies + Blondies £3
Cookies + Slices £3.50

MOCH
ADD S
Sorrel's Cocoa Bakery

el's Cocoa Bakery
FINE CHOCOLATE & BAKES
DOGS encouraged
Rocky Road

Heat & Eat Brookie Pot
Heat & Eat Brookie Pot
Heat & Eat Brookie Pot
Heat & Eat Brookie Pot
Heat & Eat Brookie Pot
Biscoff
Caramel Nutella

OAT MILK & DECA AVAILA LE
HOT CHOCOLATE 3.50
ICED COFFEE 3.00
CAPPUCCINO/LATTE 2.80
MOCHA 3.00
RUP / BISCOFF 20P

RED VELVET NUTELLA FERRERO COOKIE BARS

Preparation time: 20-35 minutes, plus 10 minutes chilling | Cooking time: 10-15 minutes | Makes 12 large chunky bars, or 24-36 bitesize chunks

Red velvet is my all-time favourite. These super indulgent, gooey cookie bars are my go-to for parties or a comforting winter night movie snack. Why not make it into a celebration cake bake? Check out our Instagram for the Nutella ganache icing recipe.

250g butter, cubed approx. 3 inch (room temp, firm but not fridge cold)
220g brown sugar
220g white sugar
640g plain flour
65g high quality cocoa powder
15g baking powder
380g white chocolate chips
3 large free range eggs
3 tsp red food colouring
½ tbsp vanilla extract
200g Nutella
200g Kinder Cream
15 Ferrero Rocher, roughly cut in half

Line a 9x12 baking tin with parchment, making sure it comes up the sides a little as you'll need these 'handles' to lift out the cookie bars. If you don't have a 9x12 don't worry! You can switch for pretty much any other size; just make sure to adjust the baking time accordingly.

Preheat your oven to 170°c (fan oven).

In your stand mixer add all of the cubed butter and the two types of sugar, then set on a medium-high speed and cream together for about 5 minutes, or until you have no lumps of butter left.

Next, mix your flour, cocoa powder, and baking powder together and then add to the mixer in thirds, making sure to scrape round the bowl between each addition. Once thoroughly combined you should have a breadcrumb texture. Now add your chocolate chips and briefly mix.

Combine your eggs, vanilla extract and red food colouring, and then add to the bowl. You want to mix for a few minutes until everything is combined, making sure that the mix at the bottom of the bowl is well incorporated too.

You should end up with soft, but not sticky, dough. Split the mixture in half and press one half into a flat layer covering the bottom of your baking tin.

Now it's time to add your fillings. Spread out Nutella and Kinder Cream in an even layer across the dough, and then scatter in your halved Ferrero Rocher. If you don't have Kinder Cream, just double up your Nutella quantities instead!

Pop in the fridge to let the fillings firm up for 10 minutes, then add the remainder of your dough as a top layer.

Bake for 9 minutes, then check. If the dough still has wet patches, bake for an extra 2-3 minutes at a time until they just disappear – if you're unsure go for slightly under baked rather than over as this will just add to the gooey texture!

You can dig in with a spoon if you can't wait, otherwise cool completely in the fridge for a couple of hours, and then slice into 12.

The perfect recipe to panic bake for that birthday you forgot about.

Tip: Store in an airtight container. These are best eaten within 4-5 days, but you can warm up and serve with ice cream for much longer.

Sorrel's Cocoa Bakery

WORD ON THE STREET

Something of an institution for The Steel City, Street Food Chef is still serving up the best burritos in town from its two shops on Arundel Street and Sharrow Vale Road.

Street Food Chef is the home of what you might describe as Tex-Mex food in Sheffield: burritos, nachos, quesadillas, and in the hot weather if you're lucky, margarita slushies! The service is canteen style at the Arundel Street shop, allowing customers to pick and choose ingredients to create the burrito of their dreams. This approach creates better interaction with customers as they can see their food being built right in front of them. There is more of a set menu at Sharrow Vale Road but each item offers plenty of options to fill and spice your meal according to personal preference.

Richard Golland is now the sole owner of Street Food Chef, having worked with his business partner Abi for many years previously. "She has decided to go on a different path," says Richard, "so I would just like to wish her all the best in whatever she takes on in the future and a big thank you for all her hard work." Since the change in leadership, Street Food Chef has focused on just two shops – dropping festivals and events – to make every experience the best it can be.

The kitchen has also spiced up its food slightly, though still offers a range of salsas to suit all palates. Meat fillings are cooked overnight for 12 hours to maximise flavour, using local producer Moss Valley's own pork and Yorkshire beef supplied by them. Packaging is kept to a minimum, using only what's needed to enable the takeaway format, such as cardboard boxes and tin foil, which has earnt the classic burrito its name: The Silver Bullet!

Although they have no plans to take over the world and will continue to stay streamlined with just the two Sheffield locations, Street Food Chef may have a few tricks up its sleeve yet... Richard has been mulling over ideas for what he dubs 'Sheff-Mex' menu items: spicing up local favourites like a chip butty, pork sandwich and even mushy peas! Amidst this innovation, he is committed to making the best burritos ever and providing great service with the help of a strong team at both shops. Richard Tulson manages the Sharrow Vale venue while Richard Golland heads up Arundel, overseeing the younger staff members.

"We all enjoy being in this industry and we want to keep serving great food to Sheffield. I grew up here and coming back 15 years ago to run this business was the best move I ever made."

CARD ONLY

elp save
he Leadmill
rom eviction
y our landlord.

EAT IN
TOASTED
Burrito
£7.45
TAKEAWAY
STREET FOOD CHEF

THE STREET FOOD CHEF
MEXICAN CANTEEN
EAT IN OR TAKEAWAY

CHICKEN TINGA

Preparation time: 15 minutes | Cooking time: 40 minutes | Serves 4

Tinga literally means stew and refers to shredded chicken, beef, or pork that stews in a combination of tomatoes, onion, garlic, chipotle peppers, and oregano.

2 tbsp olive oil
2 onions, sliced
Pinch of salt
2 large cloves of garlic, crushed
1 tsp toasted cumin seeds
2-3 tbsp chipotle chilli paste
400g tinned chopped tomatoes
Pinch of sugar
6 boneless, skinless chicken thighs
1 tsp Mexican oregano

Heat the oil in a large non-stick flameproof dish or saucepan. Fry the onions with a pinch of salt for 10 minutes, or until softened. Add the garlic and cumin and fry for 1 minute more. Tip in the chipotle paste, tomatoes, and a pinch of sugar. Half fill the tomato tin with water, swill it around, then add this to the pan.

Sit the chicken thighs in the sauce. Bring to a low simmer and cook, covered, for 20-25 minutes, stirring often, until the liquid has reduced slightly, and the chicken is cooked through.

Using two forks, shred the chicken and stir it back through the sauce. Season to taste with the Mexican oregano and salt and pepper. If the sauce is too thin, return to the heat and simmer for 5 more minutes until the sauce has reduced a little more.

You can serve this with rice or salad and top it with guacamole, sour cream and salsa.

For freezing, leave to cool completely and then transfer to large freezeproof bags.

CALIFORNIA DREAMIN'

Sheffield's newest boutique wine shop and bottle bar, Tenaya Wines, brings a taste of California to Crookes with a focus on female producers and sustainability.

Tenaya Wines was created by Sarah Hatton and Virginia Myers, who transformed a former charity shop on Crookes High Street into the stylish bottle shop and drinking space, which opened in the summer of 2022. Inspired by the West Coast of America, Tenaya combines a casual and relaxed venue with great, honest service that helps anyone find their perfect bottle of wine.

Virginia explains: "We both love California. We love the vibe and we love the produce. The people are so relaxed, open and friendly, so we want to bring a bit of that lifestyle over here. Sheffield's a naturally friendly place, so it's a good fit!" The name is also a nod to that part of the world and comes from the idyllic Tenaya Canyon, Creek and Lake in Yosemite Valley. As you might expect, the shop offers lots of Californian choices plus wines from around the world, and even a few from the burgeoning English wine scene.

Wines are available to drink in by the glass and there will be a small menu featuring reds, whites, orange, rosé and fizz to choose from. Customers can also buy any bottle from the shop and enjoy it at Tenaya for a small corkage charge, and if that wasn't tempting enough, the venue is working with Porter Brook Deli to offer accompanying snacks for build-your-own cheese and savoury picnic boards, another nod to Californian wine culture. The team are also happy to match their wines for diners heading to eat at the nearby 'byob' bistro, No Name.

Between them, Sarah and Virginia have over 20 years' experience in the wine industry, having formed a firm friendship while working together at the popular Sheffield wine shop, Starmore Boss. Virginia previously managed an independent wine shop and became a winemaker at an independent urban winery in San Francisco. Drawing on all their experience and knowledge, they want Tenaya to be an accessible, inclusive and fun destination. To this end, the vast selection of wines covers all price points and particularly celebrates female-produced wines and sustainable brands.

"We want people to feel welcome and not to feel intimidated," says Sarah. "You won't have to know a lot about wine to visit; we can help people to discover something new and find a bottle they absolutely love." Having experienced some sexism and exclusion themselves in the generally male-dominated industry, the owners of Tenaya Wines are forging a new path towards a modern, relaxed and easy way for everyone discover and enjoy their next favourite glass. Cheers to that!

tenaya
Wine Sho

MILLER'S DAMSEL
PERL LAS
GORDAL PICANTE
Perelló
MORANGIE BRIE

WINE PAIRINGS

Tenaya Wines have picked a selection of recipes elsewhere in the book and matched them with the perfect wine pairing...

Ashoka – Malai Chicken Tikka

Chaffey Bros, Kontrapunkt Kerner, Australia £20

Complex and aromatic with citrus rind, grapefruit and spicy complexity. Perfect with spicy food.

Butcher & Catch – Fish and Chip Oysters

Renishaw Hall, Sparkling White, Derbyshire, UK £27.50

A twist on the classic fish and chips/Champagne pairing, this local fizz is really classy and elegant. Bright and zippy with hints of citrus, apple and biscuits.

Chop Shop – BBQ Baby Back Ribs with Jalapeño Cheddar Cornbread

Baby Bandito, Follow Your Dreams Carignan, South Africa £21

Bright pure red berry juice, very gluggable. Herbaceous notes bring lots of complexity to this red.

Church – Vegan Mac 'n' Cheese

Ian Brand & Family, Le P'Tit Paysan, Chardonnay, Monterey, California £24

Buttery, creamy, appley and lemony with the bright acidity to bring it all together. Beautifully balanced and rich, but not too rich! Wine of dreams, perfect with Mac 'n' Cheese.

Khoo's Hot Sauce – Chilli and Lime Mexican Pork Shoulder

Dandelion, Enchanted Garden, Riesling, Australia £15

A fresh, delicate and citrusy wine with hints of white flowers and a mineral finish.

Hungry Buddha – Dal Bhat Tarkari

Călușari, Pinot Noir Rosé, Romania £9.50

A dry, fresh, fruity and easy drinking rosé. Lush notes of strawberry and a little spice on the finish.

OR Chasing Rabbits, Grenache, South Africa £18

A lush, juicy, crunchy, cherry red, chillable red!

Hungry Buddha – Momo

El Risco, Blanco, Spain £14

Crisp and refreshing Macabeo, with a lot more complexity than is often found with this grape. Lots of unctuous white peach and grapefruit peel with a subtle herbal finish.

Orange Bird – Caramelised Aubergine with Honey Labneh

La Rosita, Brut Rosé, Spain £20.50

This traditional method fizz spends 48 months on its lees so has some lovely brioche notes as well as strawberry and rosehips. Divine!

OR Flower & The Bee, White, Spain £22

A lovely full-flavoured white wine, with powerful flavours of herbs, pears and white peach. Perfect fruit intensity and amazing freshness.

PJ taste – Filo Feta Parcels with Local Honey and Beetroot Salad

Kyrenia, Roditis, Greece £16

Lemon blossom, citrus, apple and herbs. This fascinating wine has a creamy mouth texture with refreshing acidity and almost a saltiness to it.

LE P'TIT PAYSAN
RENISHAW HALL
Vintage Cuvee
2017
CĂLUȘARI
PINOT ROSE
WINE CO.
CHAFFEY
BROS.
El Risco
CALATAYUD
Dandelion Vineyards
KYRENIA
The Flower and the Bee
LA FLOR Y LA ABEJA
la rosita
brut
TRADITIONAL METHOD
produced by lobban wines, barcelona
bottled by NE 0600500 CAT
produce of spain

WINE PAIRINGS

Tenaya Wines have picked a selection of recipes elsewhere in the book and matched them with the perfect wine pairing...

PJ taste - Rack of Lamb with Local Redcurrant Jelly

Ch. Pesquié, Les Terrasses Rouge, France £16.50

A hefty, velvety, dark berry forward blend with hints of brambles and a peppery spice. A serious, cosy, wintry red.

PJ taste - Blackcurrant Sorbet with Hazelnut Crunch

Villa Cialdini, Lambrusco, Italy £17

On the nose, this sparkling red is fresh and fruity. On the palate it's delicate and tangy with lots of forest fruits and hints of flowers. Tastes best when lightly chilled!

Street Food Chef - Chicken Tinga

Susana Balbo, Crios Malbec, Argentina £13.5

Juicy cherries with notes of violet and baking spices, this medium-full bodied wine has hints of oak, but great balance.

OR Fowles - Are You Game? Shiraz, Australia £16.50

A juicy, easy-drinking Shiraz. Ripe dark plum, lightly perfumed florals, hints of vanilla oak and pepper spice. Sumptuous stuff!

Thyme Café - Beef Bourguignon

Marietta, Armé Cab Sauv Blend, California £30

Blackberries, bright cherries, plums, hints of leather and tobacco all intertwine for a wonderfully balanced mouthfeel. Sumptuous yet racy and delicious, this is quite simply a perfect, velvety Bordeaux blend.

Thyme Café - Tuscan Fish Stew

Pique & Mixe, Piquepoul-Tennet, France £11

Fresh and fruity with plenty of lemon and grapefruit as well as tropical notes and some salinity. Rich mouthfeel with a long finish. Perfect with seafood!

Thyme Café - Ras el Hanout Spiced Roast Butternut Squash

Celler de Capacanes, Cap Sentit, Spain £16

A fresh orange wine with ripe peach, apricot and floral notes. A well-rounded palate with a refreshing and bright finish. An orange wine for everyone!

True North - Curried Butternut Squash, Okra and Cashew Nut Pie

Ruth Lewandowski, Tatto Orange Wine, California £29

Vividly spicy and mouth-wateringly textured. Meyer lemons, gingery cherry pits and a bit of Muscat musk. As gluggable as it is ponderable.

Urban Choola - Nalli Gosht (Lamb Curry)

Des Andres Sisters, Garganta del Aguila, Spain £11

Sisters Ruth and Anna (Ruth studied chemistry in Sheffield!) select parcels of high altitude Garnacha to produce this soft, velvety red. Raspberry and wild strawberries with herb-like aromas such as oregano and thyme make this a fresh and vibrant red.

Susana Balbo
CRIOS
2021
MALBEC
VALLE DE UCO - MENDOZA

VILLACIALDINI

TERRASSES
2019
CHÂTEAU
PESQUIÉ

MARIETTA
ARMÉ
2019
CABERNET SAUVIGNON
MERLOT, MALBEC, PETIT VERDOT
ESTATE GROWN

GARGANTA
DEL ÁGUILA
SUELOS DE GRANITO
GARNACHA

RAIN OR SHINE, THERE'S ALWAYS THYME

Opened back in 2003, Thyme Café has gone on to firmly establish itself as one of Sheffield's favourite eateries. Since the doors first opened, the essence of Thyme has stayed the same: delicious food and drink served in an informal setting.

The unique feel of Thyme Café is complemented by an eclectic mix of handcrafted furnishings, reclaimed pews and prints from local artists celebrating Sheffield landmarks. It's these details, and a commitment to proudly serving their local community, that make Thyme so special, and keeps it consistently busy as it moves into its third decade. "We love that we have created a space where our guests instantly feel welcome, from popping in for a quick coffee and slice of cake to working lunches or hosting special celebrations with friends and family," says co-owner Kevin.

The signature wall-to-wall blackboard menus are full of British and European influenced dishes alongside café classics (regulars swear by the steak and ale pie). You will also find weekly specials and monthly changing set menus that celebrate seasonal produce. "There is a freedom afforded through having blackboards for the chefs to express themselves, and cooking with great produce from local suppliers is a real joy," says co-owner Anton.

The same focus and attention are given to the drinks offering. There is a long-standing relationship with award-winning local brewery Thornbridge, who supply a fine selection of draught beers, alongside regularly changing guest ales, cider and premium lagers. The wine list is carefully curated and matched with the dishes, which is supplemented by specials including the Thyme Café G&T, a firm favourite made to their own recipe and locally produced by Locksley Distilling Co. There is even a house blend coffee created by Forge Coffee Roasters, who are based in Kelham Island.

In addition to the main dining room with its relaxed atmosphere and open plan view of the kitchen and bar, guests can enjoy the spacious garden on sunnier days. Thyme has also opened an upstairs function room with its own bar, ideal for catered parties, functions, business meetings or private dining that still provides that same Thyme Café experience.

"There's something special about Thyme Café that makes it feel like a hub of activity in Broomhill," says co-owner Matt. "It's such an exciting place to eat, drink and work because of the creative scope we have here." Rain or shine, there's always Thyme: somewhere to sit and watch the world go by over great food and drink.

ALLERGIES & INTOLERENCES - PLEASE TALK TO STAFF ABOUT INGREDIENTS IN YOUR MEAL WHEN ORDERING

CO-LAB
THYME CAFE
ESTABLISHED 2003
LONDON DRY GIN
Botanicals: Juniper, Coriander, Angelica Root, Cassia Bark, Liquorice Root, Cassia Bark, Lemon, Thyme, Pear
A.B.V.:
40.0%
Batch/Bottle
3/32

THYME CAFE
ESTABLISHED 2003

BEEF BOURGUIGNON

Preparation time: 20-30 minutes | Cooking time: 3 hours 30 minutes | Serves 4

This is one of our favourite recipes that we always look forward to bringing back to the menu each autumn. It takes a little patience, but is worth the wait to achieve that perfect melt in the mouth texture. This is the kind of dish that brings everyone together on those darker evenings. Enjoy with friends or family and a glass of red wine from Burgundy!

1kg ox cheek, trimmed (approx. 250g per person)
300g white onion, diced
4 carrots, peeled and chopped into 2.5cm rounds
200g smoked streaky bacon, diced
4 cloves of garlic, chopped
2 tbsp tomato purée
500ml red wine
1 litre good quality beef stock (ready to use)
3 sprigs of rosemary
2 tbsp cornflour
200g chestnut mushrooms, sliced
150g baby shallots, peeled and halved
Salt and pepper
Olive oil

Season the ox cheeks with salt and pepper and then brown on all sides in a frying pan on a medium heat. Transfer to a casserole dish or deep pan.

Using the same frying pan, cook the diced onions and carrots on a medium heat until the vegetables soften. Add the streaky bacon and cook until it begins to brown.

Stir in the garlic and tomato purée to cook for 1 minute, then pour the red wine into the pan and bring to the boil. Turn down the heat and simmer for 5 minutes.

Pour this mixture over the ox cheeks in the casserole, then add the beef stock so the liquid covers the beef and drop in the rosemary.

Cover with the lid, transfer to a preheated fan oven at 160°c and cook for 3 hours. Remove from the oven, lift out the ox cheeks and place them on a plate, then put the casserole on a low heat.

Mix the cornflour with 2 tablespoons of cold water to form a paste, then whisk this into the cooking liquor. It should thicken and give the sauce a glossy appearance. If you would like it thicker, add more cornflour paste.

When you are happy with the consistency of the sauce, add the ox cheeks back to the pan and turn off the heat. Prepare the garnish by frying the sliced mushrooms and baby shallots in olive oil until softened, then stir them into the bourguignon. Serve with buttered mashed potatoes and steamed green beans.

TUSCAN FISH STEW

Preparation time: 15-20 minutes | Cooking time: 45-50 minutes | Serves 4

This is always one of our most popular dishes with guests when it is on the menu. We have suggested what fish to use, but this can be swapped with your favourite or based on what is in season. We think this offers everything in one dish and just needs some crusty bread. For a drink choice, this dish pairs well with a crisp white wine, particularly a Sauvignon.

30ml olive oil
2 white onions, diced
2 carrots, diced
2 sticks of celery, diced
1 bulb of fennel, diced
4 cloves of garlic, crushed
1 star anise
1 sprig each of thyme and rosemary
Pinch of saffron
2 tbsp tomato purée
150ml white wine
1 litre fish stock or equivalent cubes
400g fresh vine tomatoes, chopped
1 orange, juiced
400g tinned cannellini beans, drained and rinsed
200g salmon, cut into 2.5cm pieces
200g cod, cut into 2.5cm pieces
200g squid rings
200g whole prawns
2 courgettes, diced
1 lemon, juiced
5g fresh parsley, chopped
1 loaf of crusty bread
Salt and pepper

In a medium saucepan, heat the olive oil and then add all the diced vegetables, garlic, and star anise. Cook on a medium heat until all the vegetables have softened.

Add the herbs and saffron and cook for another 5 minutes, then stir in the tomato purée and cook for 2 minutes.

Add the white wine and bring to the boil, then add the fish stock and chopped tomatoes. Bring back to the boil, then simmer for 10 minutes.

Remove the pan from the heat and allow to cool for 5 minutes, then remove the star anise and use a hand blender to blitz the soup mix gently and carefully by pulsing until smooth.

Pass the soup through a sieve into a clean pan, add the orange juice and season with salt and pepper to taste. Put the pan on a medium heat, add the cannellini beans and bring to a simmer.

Add the fish, squid and prawns along with the diced courgette and simmer for 8 minutes until the pieces of fish have cooked through and are flaky.

Remove from the heat, season with a little more salt and pepper and a squeeze of lemon juice, then stir in the chopped parsley. Serve with the loaf of crusty bread on the side.

RAS EL HANOUT SPICED ROAST BUTTERNUT SQUASH

Preparation time: 25-30 minutes | Cooking time: 45-55 minutes | Serves 4

The hero ingredient in this dish is the butternut squash, with its vibrant orange flesh and sweet nutty flavour. This wholesome vegan dish is full of colour, packed with flavour and provides fibre and protein. It's great fun to create your own spice blends and they can really lift a dish; if you have some of this mix left, sprinkle it over mixed vegetables and roast them for an easy side or salad topper.

2 medium butternut squash
100ml olive oil
3 red onions, quartered
3 mixed bell peppers, quartered
240g dried quinoa (60g per person)
200g chickpeas, drained and rinsed (50g per person)
20ml red wine vinegar
10g fresh parsley
4 tsp runny honey
100g mixed seeds
400ml vegan yoghurt
½ cucumber, grated
½ lemon, zested and juiced
Salt and pepper

For the ras el hanout spice blend

1 tsp each ground cumin, coriander, ginger, black pepper and smoked paprika
¼ tsp each ground cinnamon, nutmeg and table salt

Carefully cut open the squash lengthways down the centre and scoop out the seeds. You can then either rinse and dry the seeds to be cooked in the oven on a low heat until crispy and enjoy them as a snack or use them as bird feed once fully dried.

Drizzle the squash with half the olive oil and season with salt and pepper. Place in a roasting tray, cover with foil and place in a preheated oven at 180°c for 35 minutes.

Meanwhile, prepare the onions and peppers by drizzling them with 30ml of the olive oil and seasoning with salt and pepper. Place in a roasting tray, cover with foil and place in the hot oven to cook for about 20 minutes until softened.

Rinse the quinoa and cook according to the packet instructions, then combine the quinoa with the chickpeas, red wine vinegar, remaining olive oil, and a pinch of salt and pepper. Put the lid back on the pan and leave to stand for 10 minutes, then mix in the roasted onions and peppers along with the fresh parsley.

To make the ras el hanout spice blend, simply mix all the spices and salt together until thoroughly combined. Keep this in an airtight container and it will be usable for up to 3 months.

Remove the butternut squash from the oven and check it has softened enough by pushing a fork into the flesh. It should go in easily so if there is some resistance, cook for another 10 minutes.

When the squash is softened, sprinkle each half with 2 teaspoons of your ras el hanout spice blend and then drizzle with 2 teaspoons of runny honey. Sprinkle over the mixed seeds, then return the squash to the oven and cook uncovered for a further 8 minutes.

Meanwhile, mix the yoghurt, grated cucumber, lemon zest, lemon juice and a pinch of salt and pepper together in a small bowl. Warm up the quinoa, chickpea and roast vegetable salad, then serve it with the roast spiced squash and cucumber yoghurt.

HEADING IN THE RIGHT DIRECTION

Synonymous with great pubs, pies and pints in Sheffield, True North are celebrating '30 years of us' in 2022 and business is thriving more than ever.

True North was founded in 1992 by Kane Yeardley, who is still the managing director today. He began by opening The Forum Café Bar on Division Street, which was originally an old warehouse but has remained a popular spot for food and drink overlooking Devonshire Green ever since. Over the years, True North have opened a further 13 venues including The Broadfield in Nether Edge, Riverside Kelham in Kelham Island, The Punch Bowl in Crookes, and The Waggon & Horses in Millhouses Park.

Whichever venue you visit, the focus will always be on hearty, home-cooked food that's freshly prepared with plenty of local produce. You'll find plenty of pies and other traditional pub grub on the menu, alongside True North's own beers. These are brewed just behind Forum Kitchen + Bar, on Eldon Street, in a building which stands out from the crowd thanks to a new mural painted by Rob Lee to celebrate True North's 30 year anniversary in 2022. They also created a gin and a pale ale in collaboration with Lee and will soon be releasing a limited edition 'Sheffield Champers' made with grapes grown at Renishaw Hall!

Keeping things local is what True North do best, and never more so than when they brought the much-loved Stones Bitter back to Sheffield, brewed to its original recipe on their premises. They also know how to move with the times, offering a bang up to date cocktail menu at every venue and distilling their own Sheffield Dry Gin range which was developed from scratch.

"The driving force behind everything we do is to remain a truly northern company," says marketing manager Nicky. "It's all done with the local community at heart, so when a new True North venue opens we think about how best to serve the people who are going to use it most, down to the interior design and the food offering." The team are always looking at new opportunities and exciting ways to grow their portfolio, with Kane hand-picking venues he sees True North potential in, so we can expect plenty more to come from this proudly Sheffield-based forward thinker.

DRY GIN
RHUBARB

BROADFIELD
HOTEL
TENNANTS

THE BROADFIELD'S CURRIED BUTTERNUT SQUASH, OKRA & CASHEW NUT PIE

Preparation time: 30 minutes, plus 1 hour resting | Cooking time: 1 hour | Serves 4-6

Bring the warmth of Nether Edge's favourite ale house, The Broadfield, to your home with this lightly spiced pie recipe that will conjure up cosy memories of evenings spent in the pub.

For the pastry

340g plain flour

Pinch of salt

240g butter or vegan shortening

For the filling

1 onion, chopped

1 clove of garlic, crushed

1 tsp finely chopped ginger

600g butternut squash, peeled, seeded, and cubed in thumbnail sized pieces

1 fresh chilli, seeded and finely chopped

1 tbsp garam masala

1 tsp cumin seeds

1 tin of crushed tomatoes

400g fresh okra, topped, tailed, and cut into thumbnail sized pieces

150g unsalted cashew nuts

For the pastry

Whisk the flour and salt together in a large bowl. Cut in the butter or vegan shortening with a knife or pastry blender until the mixture resembles coarse crumbs.

Add enough cold water to bring the mixture to a soft dough, one tablespoon at a time, blending gently until all the flour is moistened and the dough almost cleans the sides of the bowl.

Wrap the dough in cling film and rest in the fridge for at least 1 hour.

For the filling

Gently fry the onion, garlic, ginger and butternut squash in a little oil until they start to colour slightly.

Add the fresh chilli, garam masala and cumin seeds, then stir for a couple of minutes before adding the crushed tomato and okra.

Bring to a steady boil and then reduce the heat, cover, and leave to simmer for 15-20 minutes until the squash is cooked through. Add salt to taste. Remove from the heat and allow to cool.

While the mix is simmering, gently toast the cashew nuts in a dry frying pan until they begin to colour. Once toasted, add them to the pan with the rest of the ingredients.

While the filling cools, roll out the flaky pastry. Grease a pie tin (you could use individual pie tins or one large tin) and line with the pastry. Preheat the oven to 175°c.

Once the filling has cooled, fill the pie tin(s) and brush any exposed pastry with egg wash (optional). Cover your pie(s) with pastry lids and brush the lids with egg wash (optional).

Bake in the preheated oven for 30-35 minutes until the pastry is golden. Leave to rest for 10 minutes before serving. Enjoy!

THE THYME OF OUR LIVES

A visit to this Ecclesall Road restaurant is the perfect thyme to turnip, tune in and drop out.

Serving up refined versions of British classics, Turnip and Thyme is a cosy,home-away-from-hom on Ecclesall Road. Its friendly vibe, meticulously prepared familiar classics, and focus on locally sourced ingredients all serve to put you in safe hands, giving you ample opportunity to take a weight off and soak up the homely atmosphere.

The restaurant was set up in 2019 by Sheffield-based siblings, Rob and Louise Moore, and can be found nestled just around the corner from the picturesque Endcliffe Park.

Owners Rob and Louise both have nearly 20 years' experience working in hospitality, actually working together at four separate venues. Over those years, they often discussed putting their complementary skills to use and going it alone (well, together, but you see what we mean), so when the opportunity arose to take over the building that formerly housed Swanky's Bistro and Bar, they jumped at the chance.

With Chef Rob on cooking duties and Louise providing a warm welcome at front of house, the brother and sister duo have steadily grown a fantastic reputation for quality food and service, even picking up a couple of Good Food Awards in both 2021 and 2022.

The family affair even extends to the restaurant's quirky name, which was offered to them by their mum's friend on a list of 'terrible' puns that you'll be pleased to hear, they amended slightly.

As far as the food itself goes, their hearty menu changes seasonally and Rob describes his creations as 'homely, British comfort food', with the delicious sounding Pork Belly with Dauphinoise and a Black Pudding Croquette becoming a firm favourite with diners from day one.

Rob is passionate about local produce and sources his ingredients locally wherever possible, using the likes of Sheffield faves JH Mann on Sharrowvale Road for their fish, along with Owen Taylors butchers, who are based only a stone's throw away in Derbyshire.

Talking about the food, Rob said: "I think we offer excellent, well cooked food, done in a way that people are really enjoying. We change it with the seasons, but we try and keep to the same locally sourced, homely comfort food ethos every time."

The locally sourced ethos even extends to their drinks menu, which features exquisite gins and vodka from True North Brewery, locally roasted coffee from Forgemasters, and beer from much-loved local brewers, Abbeydale Brewery.

Not to get stuck in the mud, they also have exciting plans for the future, having recently taken on a new chef which has allowed them to open up the restaurant a few extra days a week. On top of that, they have also started taking on outside catering work.

TURNIP & THYME
NOW OPEN TUESDAY- SUNDAYS!

fresh

TURNIP & THYME
STARTERS

VENISON WELLINGTON WITH RED WINE SAUCE

Preparation time: 1 hour – 1 hour 10 minutes | Cooking time: 30 minutes | Serves 4

Autumn is a great time of year for venison, in its prime between October and January, and what better way to show it off than in a lovely Wellington! Always great paired with a sweet red wine sauce.

4 x 7oz venison haunch steaks
300g puff pastry
2 eggs

For the duxelles
100g shallots, diced
4 cloves of garlic, minced
50g unsalted butter
400g flat field mushrooms
150g baby leaf spinach
Seasoning (to taste)

For the red wine sauce
300ml red wine
1 red onion
10g rosemary
10g thyme
50g redcurrant jelly
50ml red wine vinegar
50g chicken stock
100g unsalted butter

For the vegetables
200g heirloom carrots
150g tenderstem broccoli
250g wild mushrooms
100g spinach
100g unsalted butter

For the duxelles

Sweat the diced shallots and minced garlic in butter until soft. Dice the flat field mushrooms and add to the pan, cooking everything on a high heat until the mushrooms are well cooked and drying out. Fold in the spinach and remove the pan from the heat, then leave to cool. Season as you go not all at the end!

Meanwhile, oil and season the steaks, then sear on a high heat until sealed all over but still rare, then leave to rest.

Once the duxelles and steaks are cool, cut the pastry in 4 x 75g blocks and roll each one into rectangles. Spread a layer of the mushrooms on one side, top with a steak, and then another layer of mushrooms. Using a pastry brush, egg wash the outskirts of the pastry and fold over the venison and roll. Squeeze either side of the steak so it's nice and firm then tuck in the edges, roll over and egg wash the pastry completely.

Season, and cook in the oven for 18 minutes at 180°c.

For the red wine sauce

Whilst the steaks are cooking, start making the sauce. Simply simmer all the red wine sauce ingredients apart from the butter together for 15 minutes, or until reduced by half, then strain into a clean pan. Add the butter and set the sauce aside.

For the vegetables

Just before the venison comes out of the oven, drop the carrots and tenderstem broccoli in salted boiling water, and sauté off the wild mushrooms in a frying pan. After 2 minutes, add the carrots and broccoli to the mushrooms with the butter, spinach, and seasoning.

To serve

Drizzle half the red wine sauce over the plates, arrange the vegetables over the sauce, carve the wellington in half diagonally and place over the vegetables. Pour over the remaining sauce and enjoy!

HOMEGROWN HOSPITALITY

Established over ten years ago, Urban Choola is the place to go for a true taste of authentic yet contemporary Indian cuisine in Sheffield.

The concept of Urban Choola goes back to the restaurant and takeaway's name, referring to its city location and the outdoor open fire kitchen found in traditional Indian households, known as a choola. This contrast between homestyle cooking and contemporary urban dining is what makes Urban Choola unique in Sheffield. It opened on London Road in 2012 and has since relocated to the buzzing Ecclesall Road South, but has remained true to the underlying ethos that owner Anurag began with. He felt that the true quality of Indian food wasn't well represented in the UK at the time, and decided to introduce simple, home cooked dishes that tasted just like those made by mums across India.

Homestyle cooking is still the main inspiration for developing the curries and many other dishes that feature on the à la carte, tasting, barbecue and 'urban chakna' menus. These offer guests a range of options from a set four or five course lunch to an early evening deal and even the chef's selection of tandoori dishes. Having started out with authentic Indian street food, a huge part of Urban Choola's journey has been about refinement. "We want to prove to the world what we can do with Indian food, which is normally labelled rustic or misunderstood in the UK," says Vishnu, who moved the UK himself a few years ago and was taken back by the difference between restaurants serving Indian food here and those he knew back home.

Their approach to quality has encompassed every detail of the restaurant and takeaway, from ingredients and saucing to the décor and service. Anurag and Vishnu want customers to be transported to a 'mini India' when they arrive at Urban Choola, with touches such as artwork inspired by Bollywood stars on the walls. Their aim is to be known as one of the best Indian dining hotspots not just in Sheffield but the North of England. They are also proud to be part of the city's Indian community, for whom they often host parties, weddings and other events, making them much more than just a kitchen.

"Urban Choola speaks to what Indian culture looks like through the eyes of an Indian, rather than a globalised view of our food and everything that shapes it," explains Vishnu. With each chef required to have a minimum of 10 years' industry experience, Urban Choola consistently brings the very best of Indian hospitality, society and of course its culinary magic to Sheffield.

UC
URBAN CHOOLA
SUMMER MENU
2022

URBAN CHOOLA
INDIAN RESTAURANT

COBRA

NALLI GOSHT

Preparation time: 15-20 minutes | Cooking time: 25-30 minutes | Serves 4

The irresistible Mughlai food is reminiscent of the Nawabi and the Mughal glory. The world-renowned Dum Pukht (meaning 'to breathe and to cook') cuisine owes its excellence to the fact that the food, sealed in a dish and slow-cooked in its own juices, retains its entire natural aromas and flavours.

4 green cardamom pods
2 black cardamom pods
5-6 cloves
5-6 black peppercorns
1 inch cinnamon stick
3 bay leaves
300g white onion, sliced
2 tbsp garlic paste
2 tbsp ginger paste
1 tsp red chilli powder
1 tbsp ground coriander
800g lamb leg pieces (osso buco cut)
150g tomato purée
100g yoghurt
1 tsp garam masala
Salt, to taste

Heat some vegetable oil in a thick-bottomed pan. Add the green cardamom, black cardamom, cloves, black peppercorns, cinnamon, bay leaves and sliced onion.

Sauté until the onions are lightly browned. Add the garlic paste, ginger paste, red chilli powder, and ground coriander. Cook for 1 minute, then add the lamb pieces. Give them a good stir and cook for 3 minutes on medium heat.

Add three cups of water to the pan and bring to the boil. Turn the heat down to a simmer and cook, covered, on medium heat for half an hour or until the lamb is almost cooked.

Whisk the tomato purée and yoghurt together, then add to the cooked nalli. Stir in the garam masala powder and salt, then cover and cook for a final 10 minutes.

Serve the nalli gosht hot with hot chapatis (a type of Indian bread).

If you would prefer to make this spicy, add some green chilli to taste with the garlic and ginger.

Chef's Tip: When selecting meat for this dish, make sure that you select lamb pieces with lots of bone marrow. These have to be succulent, as the spices have to seep into the marrow.

DIRECTORY

1554 COFFEE SHOP

Church Street, Sheffield, S1 1HA
07377 357563
www.1554.co.uk
1554@sheffield-cathedral.org.uk
@1554coffeeshop
We are a 100% independent coffee shop, with all proceeds supporting the work and life of Sheffield's cathedral in the heart of the city.

AESTHETE COFFEE + KITCHEN

348-352 South Road, Walkley, S6 3TE
52a Sandygate Road, Crosspool, S10 5RY
76 Barber Road, Crookesmoor, S10 1EE
0114 232 000 (Walkley)
0114 479 2000 (Crosspool)
www.aesthetesheffield.com
alexa@aesthetewalkley.com
@aesthete_sheffield
With three venues across Sheffield, Aesthete offers speciality coffee, house-made cakes and an exciting international cuisine, all inside an uplifting and welcoming environment.

AKENTANNOS

270-272 Sharrow Vale Road, Sheffield, S11 8ZH
0114 268 0505
www.akentannos.co.uk
@akentannos
A familial Sardinian restaurant on Sharrow Vale Road.

ALS GONGCHA

10 Eyre Street, Sheffield, S1 4QY
Cutlery Works, 73-101 Neepsend Lane, Sheffield, S3 8AT
0114 276 2905
@alsgongcha_sheff
Authentic Taiwanese bubble tea in a stylish café in central Sheffield and a street food stall in Cutlery Works, bringing the latest trends from East to West.

ASHOKA

307 Ecclesall Road, Sheffield, S11 8NX
0114 268 3029
ww.ashoka1967.com
One of the oldest Indian restaurants in the city, known across Sheffield for its 'reyt good curreh' and unfailingly warm welcome.

BAMBOO DOOR

Leopold Square, Sheffield, S1 2JG
0114 272 6733
www.bamboodoor.co.uk
info@bamboodoor.co.uk
@bamboo_door
Established in April 2014, Bamboo Door is Sheffield's first Tiki bar with an amazing rum selection.

BENCH

7b Nether Edge Road, Sheffield, S7 1RU
@benchsheffield
Neighbourhood bistro, bar and wine shop serving a seasonal small plate menu focused on British produce and cooking over open fire, with natural wines and cocktails from the bar.

BULLION CHOCOLATE

The Chocolate Factory, Harvest Works, Unit 7, 102-104 Harvest Lane, Sheffield, S3 8EG
& The Chocolate Shop and Café Bar, Cutlery Works, 73-101 Neepsend Lane, Sheffield, S3 8AT
0114 296 0363
www.bullionchocolate.com
hello@bullion-group.com
@officialbullion
Bullion Chocolate is a small batch bean-to-bar craft chocolate maker offering classes, factory tours, café bars and retail shops from Sheffield.

THE BULL'S HEAD

New Road, Chesterfield, S42 7EW
01246 569999
www.bullsheadholymoorside.co.uk
bookings@bullsheadholymoorside.co.uk
@the_bulls_head_holymoorside
Nestled in the heart of the Peak District, our modern cuisine awaits in a warm, friendly environment.

BUTCHER & CATCH

199-203 Whitham Road, Broomhill, Sheffield, S10 2SP
0114 263 1304
www.butcherandcatch.co.uk
contact@butcherandcatch.co.uk
@butcherandcatch
Independent seafood and steak restaurant using the very best local British produce, supporting our local farming community and helping to keep our amazing British fish landings firmly on your plates.

CHAKRA LOUNGE

5 Fitzalan Square, Sheffield, S1 2AY
0114 327 4190
www.thechakralounge.co.uk
hello@thechakralounge.co.uk
@chakraloungeofficial
From the Land of Five Rivers, Punjab, we are inspired to create soul-stirring Indian cuisine that reflects our rich history and culture.

CHINA RED

3 Rockingham Gate, Sheffield, S1 4JD
& Cutlery Works, 73-101 Neepsend Lane, Sheffield, S3 8AT
0114 272 1332
www.chinaredsheffield.com
chinaredbookings@gmail.com
@chinared_sheffield
Authentic Sichuan food in the heart of Sheffield, at the restaurant on The Moor and a street food stall in Cutlery Works.

CHOP SHOP BAR & GRILL

1b Alma Street, Kelham Island, Sheffield, S3 8RY
0114 270 6008
www.butcherandcatch.co.uk
chopshop@butcherandcatch.co.uk
@chopshopgrill
Celebrating all things meat to let the true taste of the amazing produce speak for itself, using our Argentinian asado BBQ chargrill to enhance the flavours over natural flames.

CHURCH – TEMPLE OF FUN

Osborn Works, 4a Rutland Way, Sheffield, S3 8DG
07521 610842
www.templeof.fun
info@templeof.fun
Facebook: TempleOfFun
Instagram and TikTok @TempleOf.Fun
Twitter @TempleOf_Fun
Unique vegan bar and restaurant located in Sheffield's trendy Neepsend/Kelham Island district, owned by Bring Me The Horizon frontman Oli Sykes.

CUBANA

Unit 4 Leopold Square, Sheffield, S1 2JG
0114 276 0475
www.cubanatapasbar.co.uk
@cubanatapasbar
Cubana is an independently owned tapas restaurant and Cuban bar in the beautiful surroundings of Leopold Square.

DOMO

Eagle Works, 34-36 Cotton Mill Walk, Little Kelham, S3 8DH
www.domorestaurant.co.uk
Found on the ground floor of the heritage-listed Eagle Works building in bustling Kelham Island, Domo brings a sparkling slice of Sardinian life to Sheffield.

DOUGHBOY

97 Division Street, Sheffield, S1 4GE
www.wearedoughboy.com
@wearedoughboy
Here at Doughboy, we make head-turning cookies that taste great. What started off as an artisanal small batch bakery has now grown into a multi-channel cookie concept.

DYSH COFFEE & KITCHEN

778-780 Ecclesall Road, S11 8TB
0114 266 8907
www.dyshcoffeeandkitchen.com
alice@dyshcoffeeandkitchen.com
Facebook: Dysh Sheffield
Instagram @dyshsheffield
Dysh serves all day breakfast, lunch, afternoon tea and Sunday lunch, all made in-house to be enjoyed alongside great coffee and a warm welcome.

ELM

353-355 Glossop Road, Sheffield, S10 2HP
07595 220148
www.elmsheffield.co.uk
hello@elmsheffield.co.uk
@elmsheffield
During the week Elm serve their house bagels and infamous cinnamon buns. The weekends are for sharing – meat, fish and cheese with evenings for collaborations and tastings.

FRAZER'S COFFEE

(Roastery) 47 Wilson Street, Neepsend, S3 8DD
(Coffee Shop) Castle Street, Sheffield, S3 8LN
07885 445315
www.frazerscoffeeroasters.co.uk
frazerscoffeeroasters@gmail.com
@frazerscoffeeemporium
@frazerscoffeeroasters
Frazer's Coffee Roasters is an artisan roaster started in 2014. Our main focus is on quality, fresh and great tasting coffee.

HENDERSON'S RELISH

2a Parkway Rise, Sheffield, S9 4WQ
0114 242 5724
www.hendersonsrelish.com
sales@hendersonsrelish.com
Facebook: HendersonsRelishSheffield
Instagram @hendersonsrelish
Twitter @HendoRelish
Henry Henderson blended the first batch of this famous Relish in Sheffield in 1885. More than 130 years later, we are still a family business, and are still blending our secret family recipe.

HUNGRY BUDDHA

Unit 2, Food Court, Sheffield Moor Market, Sheffield, S1 4PF
07809 476090
www.hungrybuddha.co.uk
dev_kathmandu@hotmail.com
@hungrybuddha1
Bringing home-cooked, flavoursome, subtly spiced, fresh Nepalese food to Sheffield.

INDUSTRY TAP

85 Sidney Street, Sheffield, S1 4RG
07450 897649
www.industrytap.co.uk
bar-industrytap@outlook.com
Facebook and Instagram @industrytapsheffield
Twitter @IndustrytapShef
Fab indoor and outdoor bar space serving up to 21 craft beer lines with rotating guest beers from Sheffield, the UK and beyond. Full range of wines, spirits and non-alcoholic. Available for private hire.

JAMESON'S TEAROOMS

334 Abbeydale Road, Sheffield, S7 1FN
0114 255 1159
www.jamesonstearooms.co.uk
@jamesonstearooms
We pride ourselves on our afternoon teas, home baked cakes, breakfast, brunches, delightful lunches and welcoming atmosphere.

KHOO'S HOT SAUCE

Khoo's Hot Sauce, Sheffield, S8 8QP
07961 734732
www.khooshotsauce.co.uk
info@khooshotsauce.co.uk
@khooshotsauce
Khoo's Hot Sauce is a proud producer of high-quality artisan chilli sauces forged in the Steel City.

KNAB FARM SHOP

78 Montrose Road, Sheffield, S7 2EF
0114 250 7144
www.knabfarmshop.co.uk
knabfarmshop@outlook.com
@knab_farm_shop
We are a local community store providing groceries, fruit and vegetables, baked goods and local beer and wine. We are a truly independent business, owned by a local family.

KOMMUNE

Castle House, Angel Street, Sheffield, S3 8LS
www.kommune.co.uk
info@kommune.co.uk
Facebook: kommune.ch
Instagram @kommune_ch
TikTok @kommunech
Twitter @kommune_ch
Bringing together some of the most exciting independent kitchens and traders from across the country, Kommune is a social all-day dining and retail experience, situated in a unique Grade II listed building at the very heart of Sheffield.

KONJŌ

Cutlery Works, 73-101 Neepsend Lane, Sheffield, S3 8AT
sheffield@konjokitchen.co.uk
Facebook: konjokitchen
Instagram @konjokitchen
East Asian inspired fast food.

LA MAMA

238 Abbeydale Road, Nether Edge, Sheffield, S7 1FL
0114 327 9597
www.lamamalatin.co.uk
lamama.latin@gmail.com
@lamama_tapasbar
Family-run restaurant offering small plates of Spanish/Latin American dishes, plus live music.

LOCKSLEY DISTILLING CO. LTD.

Unit 20C-1 Portland Works, Sheffield, S2 4SJ
0114 249 0359
www.locksleydistilling.com
info@locksleydistilling.com
Facebook: Sir Robin of Locksley Gin
Instagram @locksleydistilling
Twitter @locksleystill
The uncompromising quest to be the best is at the heart of Locksley's core values.

LUCA

9 Langsett Road South, Sheffield, S35 0GY
07543 133369
www.lucarestaurants.co.uk
hello@lucarestaurants.co.uk
Contemporary casual dining with a Mediterranean twist. Fully licenced with an extensive wine list and internal craft beer selection.

MITCHELLS WINE MERCHANTS

354 Meadowhead, Sheffield, S8 7UJ
0114 274 5587
www.mitchellswine.co.uk
infó@mitchellswine.co.uk
@mitchellswine
Renowned departmental store with a unique array of products including wines, beers, whisky, cigars, spirits and much more with regular tasting events and a delivery service.

MOSS VALLEY FINE MEATS

Povey Farm, Lightwood Lane, S8 8BG
0114 239 9922 / 07976 434206
www.mossvalleyfinemeats.co.uk
srt@mossvalleyfinemeats.co.uk
@mossvalleyfinemeats
Moss Valley Fine Meats is a butchery that offers award-winning pork, sausages and bacon. The farm is family run, with the fourth generation now farming here.

NORTH TOWN DELI & KITCHEN

701 Abbeydale Road, Nether Edge, Sheffield, S7 2BE
0114 255 1242
www.northtown.store
hello@northtown.store
@northtownkitchen
Bringing contemporary Italian style cookery to the heart of Sheffield. North Town boasts honest, hearty and healthy fare.

OMEGA AT ABBEYDALE

Abbeydale Sports Club, Abbeydale Road South, Sheffield, S17 3LJ
0114 236 7011
www.omegaatabbeydale.co.uk
info@omegaatabbeydale.co.uk
Facebook: Omega at Abbeydale
Twitter @OmegaAbbeydale
Restaurant, bar, and function room in the pavilion of a sports club, offering an ideal venue for corporate and private events in the south of Sheffield.

ORANGE BIRD

78 Middlewood Road, Hillsborough S6 4HA
0114 234 9330
www.theorangebird.co.uk
reservations@theorangebird.co.uk
Facebook: orangebirdkitchen
Instagram @theorangebirdkitchen
Twitter @theOrangeBird2
Orange Bird is a compact, buzzing neighbourhood restaurant and bar in the heart of Hillsborough. Our food is modern South African, cooked on a braai.

PJ TASTE LTD

54 Staniforth Road, Sheffield, S9 3HB
0114 312 3663
www.pjtaste.co.uk
ask@pjtaste.co.uk
Serving seasonally inspired local food for large corporate dinners, weddings and events in Sheffield since 2006.

SHEFFIELD DRAGON LTD

Dobcroft Road, Sheffield, S7 2LS
07985 155715 / 0114 262 0860
www.sheffielddragon.com
andrew@sheffielddragon.com
Facebook: Sheffielddragon
Instagram @the.sheffield.dragon_insta
Uniquely tasty chilli pickles and hot sauces, from reyt tasty to reyt hot and tasty!

THE SHEFFIELD HONEY COMPANY

Nethercliffe Barn, Hill Top, Stannington, Sheffield, S6 6GW
07980 261554
www.sheffield-honey.co.uk
info@sheffield-honey.co.uk
Facebook, Twitter, and YouTube @ SheffieldHoney
Instagram @sheffield.honey
The Sheffield Honey Company is a British based award-winning artisan producer of premium quality local English honey and the finest beeswax products.

SMITH & TISSINGTON

Stall 30-31, The Moor Market, 77, The Moor, Sheffield, S1 4PF
0114 272 2783
mattiss@btinternet.com
@SmithTissington
Smith & Tissington is a family business in The Moor Market, focusing mainly on fresh fish, fresh shellfish, seafood, frozen produce and eggs.

SORREL'S COCOA BAKERY

158 Crookes Road, Sheffield, S10 1UH
www.sorrelscocoabakery.com
hello@sorrelscocoabakery.com
@sorrelscocoabakery
Luxe handmade chocolates, brownies, cookies, and all things sweet.

STREET FOOD CHEF

90 Arundel Street, Sheffield, S1 4RE
376 Sharrow Vale Road, Sheffield, S11 8ZP
0114 275 2390 (Arundel)
0114 327 4778 (Sharrow)
www.streetfoodchef.co.uk
arundel@streetfoodchef.co.uk
sharrow@streetfoodchef.co.uk
@streetfoodchef
The home of Mexican food in Sheffield with delicious burritos, nachos, quesadillas and more available to eat in at Arundel or take away at both shops.

TENAYA WINE

239-241 Crookes Road, Sheffield, S10 1TF
07543 792379
www.tenayawine.co.uk
hello@tenayawine.co.uk
@tenaya_wine
A neighbourhood wine shop and bar providing an interesting and accessible range of wines with a focus on female producers and sustainability.

THYME CAFÉ

490 Glossop Road, Broomhill, S10 2QA
0114 267 0735
www.thymecafe.co.uk
bookings@thymecafe.co.uk
Facebook: thymecafesheffield
Instagram @thymecafes10
Delicious food and drink served in an informal setting with signature blackboard menus celebrating seasonal produce.

TRUE NORTH BREW CO.

47 Eldon Street, Sheffield, S1 4GX
0114 272 0569
www.truenorthbrewco.uk
info@truenorthbrewco.uk
@truenorthbrewco
Celebrating 30 years in 2022, True North are synonymous with great pubs, pies, and pints in Sheffield.

TURNIP AND THYME

740 Ecclesall Road, Sheffield, S11 8TB
0114 266 1510
www.turnipandthyme.co.uk
info@turnipandthyme.co.uk
@turnipandthyme
Created by brother and sister duo Robert and Louise, Turnip and Thyme serves British favourites and comfort food classics. We emphasise using seasonal and locally sourced ingredients.

URBAN CHOOLA LTD.

842 Ecclesall Road, Sheffield, S11 8TD
0114 266 6681
www.urbanchoola.com
info@urbanchoola.co.uk / booking.choola@gmail.com
Facebook: Urban Choola
Instagram @urban_choola
Urban Choola serves authentic Indian cuisine with a contemporary twist and honours high-quality, fresh, seasonal ingredients that are as nutritious as they are delicious. True to our philosophy, dishes are well composed, made from fresh produce, finely spiced, and full of flavour.